Otherwise Normal People

Otherwise Normal People

*Inside the Thorny World
of Competitive Rose Gardening*

Aurelia C. Scott

ALGONQUIN BOOKS OF CHAPEL HILL   2007

Published by
Algonquin Books of Chapel Hill
Post Office Box 2225
Chapel Hill, North Carolina 27515-2225

a division of
Workman Publishing
225 Varick Street
New York, New York 10014

Library of Congress Cataloging-in-Publication Data
Scott, Aurelia, C.
Otherwise normal people : inside the thorny world of
competitive rose gardening / by Aurelia C. Scott. — 1st ed.
p. cm.
Includes bibliographical references.
ISBN-13: 978-1-56512-464-6 (hardcover)
1. Rose breeders — United States — Biography.   2. Roses —
Breeding — United States — Anecdotes.   3. Rose culture — United
States — Anecdotes.   4. Scott, Aurelia C.   I. Title.
SB411.4.S36 2007
635.9'33734092273 — dc22   2006027489

10 9 8 7 6 5 4 3 2 1
First Edition

This book is dedicated to my husband,
Bob Krug, who makes all things possible

And to the memory of the women
who gave me roses —
My mother,
Carmalita Foster Benson Scott
1929 – 2005
and
My grandmother,
Mary Carmalita Lewis Benson
1899 – 1971

Won't you come into the garden?
I would like my roses to see you.

—Richard B. Sheridan,
1751 – 1816

Contents

Prologue

MENTION ROSES in Portland, Maine, and someone will ask, "Do you know the man on Capisic Street?" Mention Portland, Maine, at a meeting of rose lovers and someone will ask, "Do you know Clarence Rhodes?"

When I called Clarence, he said, "Sure, you can come talk about roses. If I don't answer the door, you'll find me out back." I found him shredding leaves for compost.

Ten minutes after he turned off the shredder and started to talk, I knew that the subject of this book would be the people of the rose world. These are gardeners for whom 'Butterscotch' is a large-flowered light orange climber, not an ice-cream topping; 'Mr. Chips' is not Robert Donat, or even Peter O'Toole, but a hybrid tea that flowers repeatedly in a Tequila Sunrise–like blend of yellow, orange, and pink.

With Clarence as my guide, I met collectors who strive to possess every class of rose and specialists infatuated with a single variety. I watched exhibitors enter prize specimens in national competitions and toured greenhouses with breeders who dream of an elusively perfect bloom. I listened to historians argue about the provenance of America's first roses. And I nodded as one seemingly rational person after another explained how their collection of three or five or nine roses had grown to three hundred, six hundred, even one thousand plants.

"Rose people are crazy," explained Clarence as he devised a long-handled spray wand with which to douse his two hundred hybrid teas.

This book is about such impassioned gardeners. They bury their tender roses in deep pits in autumn and dig them up in spring. They warn underperforming roses of impending doom by leaving a sharp shovel lying about. They lose marriages because of roses. They find love through roses. They collect roses as omnivorously as they once collected dolls and baseball cards.

These are gardeners who grow tender roses in the frigid North and disease-prone roses in the humid South simply for the challenge. They decorate otherwise lovely yards with paper bags and panty hose to isolate their choicest specimens. They traipse through overgrown fields in the worst weather to save antique roses from extinction. Twice a year, the most competitive rose people cut the prettiest blossoms off their best plants, take them to a national convention, and groom them for seven hours in order to contend for the highest honor.

America's roseaholics own more pruners, snippers, short sharp knives, and long leather gloves than most people. And, just like Clarence, they squish Japanese beetles between their fingers for the sheer pleasure of killing the enemy.

Otherwise Normal People

1

Clarence's Containers

Clarence Rhodes's front door is blocked by the copper blossoms of 'Playtime'. The path leading up to the door is barricaded by peach 'Marilyn Monroe' and mauve 'Cologne'. His short two-car driveway is so narrowed by apricot, pink, and scarlet blooms that his Chevy Astro van barely fits between the flowering walls. And the garage? For six months of the year, it's full of gardening paraphernalia. For the rest of the year, it's full of roses.

Clarence Rhodes has the round lined face of a midwestern corn farmer and the rolling infectious laugh of the Wizard of Oz after his secret was discovered. Clarence's own secret is evident to anyone who has ever seen the floral display that almost hides his gray-shingle cape on a tree-lined residential street. He is simply wild about roses. So wild that he grows two hundred tender hybrid teas in cutoff ten- and twenty-gallon plastic trash containers and about fifty hardier varieties in the ground beside his back patio. He is immoderate perhaps, but if you know that the root of the name Rhodes is *rhodon*, the Greek word for rose, his passion seems inevitable.

I also grow roses. But I live in downtown Portland and raise only two winter-hardy 'Henry Kelsey' climbers amid other perennials in my postage-stamp yard. I planted them to honor my cousin Kelsey, who lives three thousand miles away. When the late June sun warms the merlot blossoms' spicy scent, I inhale with gratitude. Yet I don't love these roses more than my 'Munstead' lavender or 'Mount Fuji' phlox. So I have driven out to tree-lined Capisic Street to meet Clarence. I want to understand his passion.

Clarence's story begins with the love of a husband for his wife. "When we moved from Cleveland, Ohio, to Portland, Maine, in 1968, my wife thought that we were moving to the end of the world." Clarence is both amused by the ridiculousness of her thought and appreciative of its accuracy. To cheer her up, he came home one day with twelve rosebushes. Clarence is as thrifty as he is thoughtful, so he collected bricks from a neighborhood school that was being demolished and built a patio off the back door. Beside it, he planted the roses. It was summer and a heady scent drifted in the kitchen window; his wife, Phyllis, unpacked her bags.

Phyllis appreciated the flowers, but she enjoyed people more than plants. So when he spotted a notice for a Maine Rose Society meeting, off they went.

"Our first year in the Maine Rose Society, I met a man who lived up in Livermore Falls. Know where that is?" I nod. Livermore Falls is north of Portland near the Maine – New Hampshire border; it is deep in ski country.

"Well, that guy grew six hundred roses. Six hundred roses in a place where winter lasts through May! I thought, 'There's a man who likes a challenge.'" As Clarence heads out to a shredder that's set up near a massive compost bin at the end of his property, I hear him say, "I like a challenge, too."

In a trice, it seems, he and Phyllis joined the American Rose

Society (ARS), a national organization founded in 1892 to promote the cultivation and enjoyment of roses. It is the largest specialized plant society in the country. They joined two local ARS societies as well and soon were traveling to California, Oregon, and England to attend national and international rose conventions. By way of explanation, Clarence says, "Everybody has to do something." And then, "You get involved."

With that he switches on the thundering shredder and directs me to pour an oversized paper bag of leaves into its maw as he pushes them through with a stick. When the last of the leaves has joined the drifting pile of brown confetti at our feet, Clarence shuts off the machine. He wears work-stained khakis, lace-up work boots, and a white T-shirt topped with a pink long-sleeved thermal undershirt covered by a baby blue long-sleeved Polo shirt finished with a deep pink wool cardigan. A bright blue nylon feed cap covers close-cropped white hair. The lenses of his horn-rimmed glasses are coated in a chaff of shredded leaves and grass.

A wiry man appears suddenly at the top of the yard pushing a wheelbarrow loaded with rose cuttings. He has the narrow, granite-serious face of Yankee legend. His red and black checked wool jacket flaps open as he pushes the top-heavy load around a towering spruce tree.

"Just dump it there, Howard." Clarence gestures toward a spot to the left of the shredder. Without speaking, he dumps and trundles his rattling, empty wheelbarrow away.

"Pruning his sister's roses. He'll be back."

Howard did return three times that afternoon; each time pushing quietly up the hill, tipping and departing without smiling, speaking, or for that matter, despite his advanced years, breathing hard. Why waste unnecessary words when you both know what you are about? And when Clarence is talking to a woman you don't know, why interrupt?

We stand at the top of the backyard slope beside the silenced shredder, looking down past the sixteen-hundred-square-foot vegetable garden to the riot of color that encircles Clarence's home. Over 150 roses rainbow around the back of the gray-shingled house — apricot 'Midas Touch' jostles cream and pink 'Gemini'; pale lemon 'Elena' glimmers beside coral-blend 'Briga-doon', whose piquant scent Clarence had wanted me to inhale as we'd walked by.

"I have the best soil in Portland." He gestures toward a home-made green wooden compost bin beside the shredder. "That's why." The bin holds at least thirty oversized wheelbarrow loads of compost.

You don't want to put rose-cutting compost onto roses, as it might spread disease. So the compost made of cuttings, all thirty wheelbarrows of it, gets forked into the vegetable garden every spring where it helps to create the deep, dark, worm-wriggling soil at the end of Clarence's spade.

"I don't use a tiller; do it all by hand. That's my exercise." Clarence will be seventy-six on his next birthday. "Let me show you another pile of stuff."

We walk over to a second compost system, this one made of two-inch-thick boards bolted together to create a three-bin sixteen-by-four-foot container. I have been admiring this con-struction since I arrived. I teach a composting course at Portland Adult Education and am always looking for inspired compost systems to show my students. This one runs along the left side of Clarence's yard, separating his land from his neighbor's. He has graded the container to stay level despite the slope of the hill and flanked it with roses. It is a Rolls Royce of compost bins. It is beautiful.

Clarence agrees. "Nothing nicer than good looking compost."

Inside the bins, he has sixteen feet of the best compost I have ever seen. He digs a short-fingered, muscled hand into the uppermost bin and stirs up a mass of what looks like damp, finely broken leaves. "This summer's leaves and grass; nothing else. I shred it, dump it in, and leave it be."

I make astonished noises. He nods.

"Some people turn their compost. I believe that's a matter of how much ambition you have. I prefer to wait."

"Let the worms do your work?" I ask.

"That's it."

The center bin holds last year's leaves and grass, and the third bin contains gardener's gold: three-year-old bittersweet-chocolate-colored, leaf-mold compost. Not an exorbitantly priced little plastic bag of preciousness, you understand, but loads of the stuff. He uses it to mulch his roses, or, as he says, "dress them up a bit."

"We went to the Spring National Rose Show the first year we belonged to the American Rose Society. Our first trip to California. The roses there were unbelievable. The color, the size, the . . ." He trails off in remembered wonder, then gives his sturdy shoulders a shake. "So I decided to see if I could grow California roses here. That's what I call any big, colorful hybrid tea — a California rose."

Hybrid tea shrubs are the traditional florist's rose with large, urn-shaped blossoms on long stems. This class, or group of roses, originated in 1867, when the House of Guillot in Lyons, France, crossed a tender tea rose with the sturdier hybrid perpetual and created the largest and most popular class of roses of all time. 'La France', which had intensely fragrant, silvery pink blossoms, is recognized as the first rose to combine the delicate petals and ever-blooming habit of tea roses with the large blooms and sturdy growth of hybrid perpetuals. The ARS *Handbook for Selecting Roses* gives 'La France' only an average rating, but if you want to grow a piece of history, it's available from nurseries that specialize in old-garden roses, or OGRs.

Hybrid teas bloom continuously through the growing season and come in a peacock array of colors. In an effort to breed ever brighter blossoms, hybridizers have often sacrificed scent, which is a recessive factor easily lost in cross-breeding. As a result, unlike 'La France', many modern hybrid teas have no perfume. Clarence, though, loves the sweet aroma of old-fashioned roses, even though he doesn't like the old roses themselves. So when each year's catalogs thump through his mail slot, he pours over them in search of new hybrid teas with nineteenth-century perfume.

The enormous number of bare-root hybrid teas sold by local nurseries and chain retailers demonstrate their lasting popularity, yet many are only semihardy, which means that they need winter protection in cold-weather climates. Growing "California" hybrid teas in Portland, Maine, where winter lows can dip to – 20 degrees F demands imagination, precision, and orneriness.

Clarence knew that desiccation kills faster than cold, so he built long containers to cover his tender roses using a product that soaked up and released atmospheric moisture. This ensured that plants inside the containers never dried out.

He hands me a six-inch remnant of the Styrofoam-like product. "It only lasts a few years, though, and I decided that it was too expensive to keep buying. Or maybe they stopped making it. I can't remember. Anyway, I had to find another solution."

He made tunnels covered with heavy duty plastic. The plastic tunnels were too hot on sunny winter days. His roses fried.

He built long containers of pressure-treated board and plywood that he anchored with weighted ropes.

"Here!" He lifts a weighted rope from a collection in his work shed at the top of the garden. "Made them exactly the right length to drape from one side over to the other with the weights barely touching the ground." Clarence is a retired electrical field-service engineer. He loves to solve problems, but this wasn't the solution. His roses shriveled from dehydration.

The next year, he covered the hybrid teas with leaves collected from his neighbors before covering the plants and the leaves with the wood-and-plywood tunnels. That year, the roses lived.

"The thing is, my wooden tunnels are heavy and they are only twenty-four inches high. Every winter, I have to prune my roses back severely to fit inside the containers. Can't make the containers bigger or I'd never be able to carry them around." He steps out of the shed. "I want to grow roses like I saw that first time in California. Huge roses!" He lifts a hand to shoulder height to demonstrate.

He tried planting his roses in whisky barrels that could be wheeled into the protection of the garage for the winter. He could grow tender hybrid teas as big as he wanted, but the whisky barrels were a back-straining pain to move.

"And they fall apart after ten years," he adds.

The eureka moment arrived nine years ago in Home Depot. He was on his way to the lumber department when he walked by a display of gray forty-gallon Rubbermaid rolling trash bins.

Most people see garbage container. Clarence saw lightweight, nonrotting, wheeled rose container. He bought six.

Today he has thirty-six. He transforms them into twenty-gallon containers by cutting off the top half. He drills drainage holes, fills the containers with a mixture of peat moss, vermiculite and perlite marketed as ProMix BX, plants them with the most vibrant hybrid teas he can find, tops the planting mix with a dressing of compost, and sets the pots in front of his house where they stop traffic.

One bag of ProMix fills two containers. Each container costs fifty dollars. Clarence is as thrifty as any Mainer by way of Maryland and Ohio can be. After a few years he switched to less expensive ten-gallon black plastic containers. They are almost as durable. One bag of ProMix fills four. And the plants grow just as well.

"It's just that they have no wheels," muses Clarence, momentarily downcast as we survey the forest of container roses in front of his house.

With or without wheels, in early December he moves all two hundred containers from the yard into the garage where they stay until the last week of March, when he rolls them back out into the driveway. Storing his hybrid teas inside keeps them alive and reduces the need for drastic pruning. The protection also gives him a week's head start on the season.

"June is the big rose show month," he explains. "This far north you need all the help you can get."

A rose show is a competitive staging of roses grown by amateur exhibitors in their own gardens. It is the floral equivalent of a dog show. Instead of grooming and showing canines, rose exhibitors groom cut flowers to the peak of perfection and display them to the public in judged competition.

Such shows are an English import. The National Rose Society of Britain held its first one in 1858. Thirty years later rose enthusiasts in Portland, Oregon, followed suit. In 1913 the ARS began to help local rose societies manage their competitive exhibitions, and in October 1935, in San Diego, California, the ARS hosted its first national show.

The ARS now sponsors three national shows a year — Spring, Fall, and All-Miniature — and helps coordinate the annual competitions organized by over four hundred affiliate local societies and the districts that oversee them. As its name implies, the ARS All-Miniature, held in midsummer, is devoted exclusively to miniature varieties. Minis are three- to eighteen-inch-high plants with correspondingly tiny blossoms. Exhibitors at the ARS Spring and Fall Nationals may show any of the tens of thousands of existing named varieties within the thirty-five classes, or categories, of roses recognized by the ARS. However, only hybrid teas — the type that Clarence grows — are eligible to win the top awards of Queen, King, Princess, and Best of Show. An exhibitor such as Clarence could conceivably enter blooms in every local show within the district, the district show, and all three national shows. Rose-growing weather is fickle, though, and transporting cut flowers long distances is chancy. Most exhibitors enter three to five shows a year.

Clarence is not a national exhibitor, but he attends national shows, which are held in different locations each year, in order to visit gardens and stay in touch with his wide circle of rosarian friends. He also goes so that he can watch top exhibitors groom and show the newest varieties. Occasionally, he serves as a judge or teaches a technical seminar during the convention.

He does exhibit in local and district shows. Recently he transported ninety cut blooms to an ARS Yankee District show on Cape Cod. He also took a five-foot 'Love and Peace' shrub to an ARS Fall National in Washington, DC, where its size, glossy leaves, and bright red-rimmed yellow blooms confounded other growers.

"Until they walked up close, they thought it was a fake." He adds that 'Love and Peace' flowers are too garish for his taste, but he features it in his sidewalk display because it's such a car stopper. A natural showman, then, if not a national exhibitor.

Exhibitors do it for the glory. There is no money in showing roses — no cash awards, no endorsement contracts for Felco pruners. Prizes range from crystal bowls and silver-plated candlesticks to paintings of roses and engraved wooden plaques. Some major awards, such as the Spring National's Joseph J. Kern Trophy, are represented by massive crystal vases and gold-trimmed urns. But these prizes may be kept by the winner only until the next show and they cost so much to insure that most exhibitors content themselves with a framed certificate that is theirs to keep.

Instead of money and valuable prizes, exhibitors battle for the thrill of the win. Their delight in winning is certainly heightened by the pleasure of beating their competitors. After all, they have just spent hours grooming their blooms for the show in a room full of colleagues determined to defeat them. But in its purest sense, winning also represents individual excellence. Like golfers who trek the links alone in bad weather, driving and putting toward perfection, exhibitors strive to create the most perfect bloom for its own sake. They love the challenge of doing something difficult well, and doing it better than other people. They are rewarded by the affirmation of their superior rose-growing and rose-grooming skill, and with fame within the rose-crazy community.

Rose shows are popular worldwide. The World Federation of Rose Societies currently includes thirty-six member countries. As you might expect, Canada, Great Britain, South Africa, and the United States are members, but the federation also includes societies from such dissimilar locations as Pakistan, Slovenia, and Uruguay. All member countries have rose societies that host competitive shows, and most welcome any exhibitor willing to pay the entrance fee and fly their blossoms around the world.

Other people devoted to one species, such as orchid or dahlia enthusiasts, also stage public shows. Yet rose lovers hold larger and more frequent events than any other group. They also are more likely to have a single-species garden than other plant aficionados — in other words, they are more likely to grow only roses than a rhododendron specialist is to raise only rhodos. Stephen Scanniello, the man who made the Brooklyn Botanic Garden's Cranford Rose Garden into a must-see venue, says that "roses are the only plant that is varied enough to comprise an entire garden."

In part, this is simply because there are so many types of roses. The ARS recognizes thirty-five rose classes, or groups of roses that share common characteristics. Within each class are hundreds, sometimes thousands, of individual named varieties, such as the floribunda 'Iceberg' or the climber 'New Dawn'. One Web site has compiled an extensive, but not exhaustive, list of the best-known. It currently contains over twenty-eight thousand varieties, including 1,993 hybrid perpetuals, a large scented shrub that first became popular during the nineteenth century. Over nine thousand unique hybrid teas appear, and almost four thousand floribunda, a continuously blooming cluster-flowered plant that resembles a hybrid tea.

The rose is more geographically adaptable; appears in more sizes, colors, shapes, and blossom types; and blooms over a longer period than any other flowering plant. Like Scheherazade, she tells a thousand tales, captivating us by adapting to our desire. If we wish, she will become an unscented five-petal pink micro-mini that fits on an indoor windowsill, or she can transform herself into a fifty-petal apricot climber that envelopes the front porch in a swoon of fragrance. It is almost impossible to resist the wiles of such a chameleon, and it's doubtful we have ever tried. Rose passion is as ancient as the plant that inspires it.

THE ROSE IS NATIVE to the world's Northern Hemisphere, which means that it ranges naturally throughout North America, Europe, Asia, India and the northern two-thirds of the African continent. While they prefer temperate climes, roses are tough; they have been found blooming in such disparate locations as Greenland and the Sahara. Scientific study of rose chromosomes and of the distribution of old rose species indicate that this scented band may well have originated with just one — the Mother of All Roses. So far, we don't know where that rose grew, but we can guess. Over half of the two hundred or so known wild rose species are native to China. So it seems likely that the mother of all our roses first grew on a Chinese plain.

The National Park Service Web site features photographs of thirty-four-million-year-old fossil roses found in Colorado. They're remnants of the lush flora that once thicketed an Oligocene-era lake. The charcoaled impression of a bud in pale pink shale is less than a half inch wide and slightly over a half inch tall. This may or may not mean that the earliest rose plants were small. After all, many large wild rose shrubs produce a welter of tiny blossoms. Unless we find an entire plant fossilized in an ancient sandbank, we'll never know. However, one can say that despite its diminutive size, the rosebud is identifiably, reassuringly itself. It sits forthrightly atop a round hip from which bristles emanate.

Our ancestors had to wander out of central Africa before they found the rose. Once they did, it was probably love at first sight, scent — and taste, for the hips, or fruits, of many varieties are as sweet as they are nutritious. Rutgers University geneticist Terry McGuire hypothesizes that early agricultural societies saved the prettiest wildflowers when they cleared land for planting. Gradually, such societies moved from preserving pretty flowers — and roses are certainly pretty — to cultivating them.

"Because they are a source of pleasure — a positive emotion inducer — we take care of them," McGuire says. "In that sense they're like dogs. They are the pets of the plant world."

By 5000 BCE, the Sumerians of Mesopotamia had written about their floral pets. By 3000 BCE, the Chinese were cultivating them. By 1500 BCE, a Minoan artist on Crete had painted the first known portrait of a rose. Visitors can still see the stylized six-petal, salmon pink rose beside a gray-winged dove on a fresco at the Palace of Knossos. Although older floral illustrations do exist, particularly Egyptian funerary paintings of the lotus from about 2000 BCE, the Knossos rose is one of the earliest flower paintings to appear decorative rather than religious. It seems to have been painted purely for the pleasure of its image. Around the same time in Persia, which was known as "Land of the Roses," the rose was sanctified as Queen of All Flowers.

Ancient Romans may have loved the Queen more than any other early culture. In Rome May 23 was Rosalia Day, when the locals tossed rose petal confetti in the streets, drenched themselves in rose oil, dressed in shades of rose, ate rose-flavored food, and guzzled rose-flavored beer and wine. In fact, rose-flavored wine was so generally popular that the Roman legions once staged a fight strike after arriving in Gaul to find that their wine was the unscented kind. To meet the demand for petals in food, cosmetics, and medicine, Romans established public rose gardens and commercial rose farms throughout the empire. They often managed to force two bloom cycles a year by growing roses in greenhouses and irrigating them with warm water. By spreading roses throughout the empire, they inculcated the conquered with a love of roses, if not a love of Romans.

Roman excesses and their emperors' tendency to throw Christians to the lions caused the early Christian church to discourage the use of roses. Yet despite official disapproval, the flower remained popular. By the sixth century the Christian church succumbed to the will of the people and began to bestow the rose with religious significance. It became a symbol of the blood of martyrs; the five-petal red rose, an emblem of Christ's five wounds; and the white rose, a sign of his mother's purity. Monastery gardens all over Europe and Great Britain grew roses. Early rosaries were counted on 165 dried, rolled-up rose petals.

Meanwhile, the rise of the Arabian Empire in the eighth century fostered the rose's flowering in the rest of Europe and Asia Minor. After discovering the flower while conquering Persia, Arabs carried their new favorite with them throughout their empire, which spanned India, North Africa, and Spain. Images of roses adorned their intricate mosaics, fabrics, and carved wooden window screens. Attar of roses, or rose oil, mixed with rose petals scented and colored bath water. Rose water was known as "the dew of paradise." And it is said that when the prophet Mohammad rose to heaven, drops of his sweat fell to earth as roses.

As the Greek poet Sappho famously wrote:

> Would you appoint some flower to reign
> In matchless beauty on the plain,
> The Rose (mankind will all agree),
> The Rose the Queen of Flowers should be.

Amid the floral bounty of Clarence's garden, I begin to understand what Sappho meant. After an hour among the roses, I don't notice the large gray containers anymore. I see only the vibrant flurry above them. And I inhale the fragrance. Clarence bends a cardinal bloom toward me — 'Ingrid Bergman' — the scent captivates.

The source of that aroma, attar of roses, remains the precious commodity that it was in eighth-century Arabia. Ten thousand acres of *Rosa damascena* 'Trigintipetala', the base note for many of the world's perfumes, blush Bulgaria's Kazanlik Valley. Attar is harvested in an exacting process that begins with the collection of rose buds between the hours of sunrise and 10 a.m. during the months of May and June. Sounds superstitious, yet centuries of practice have taught the farmers that buds must be gathered just as they begin to pink and before the essential oils weaken. They are distilled immediately upon harvest. One million buds produce three tons of flowers that condense into two and a half pounds of attar.

Clarence has lived alone with this beauty since 1992, when Phyllis died. That had been the year that he planned to retire. Without her, he worked for another year and then left engineering for a full-time life with the Queen of Flowers. The Maine Rose Society created the Phyllis and Clarence Rhodes Friendship Trophy, which is awarded at the Maine Rose Show to a winning arrangement of three sprays of floribunda, a hardy class of shrubs created in the 1930s. What had begun as a way to make his wife happy, and continued as a shared interest, has become a singular passion.

"It keeps me busy," he says.

Despite his devotion to compost, Clarence is no organic gardener. Like the majority of exhibition-class rose growers, he uses an armada of chemical weapons to keep the plants in bloom and the bugs and diseases at bay. He just uses them in addition to cultivating a fertile, compost-rich soil and applying environmentally safe amendments, such as liquid seaweed. He uses high phosphorus fertilizer to promote lavish bloom. Pesticides kill aphids, thrips, and Japanese beetles. Fungicides battle black spot and powdery mildew. He experiments constantly with mixes and ratios. And when all else fails, he blasts the roses with Malathion, which asks users to wear a full-face mask during application or risk dizziness, confusion, and nausea.

Clarence discovers new products every year at the ARS Spring and Fall Nationals, where he talks to colleagues about what works for them and collects shopping bags full of free samples hawked by rooms full of vendors. When he finds an effective product, he orders it by the case, because "they're always finding out that this stuff can be dangerous and then they stop making it." He sounds aggrieved.

To distract him from the half-empty brown container of recently banned substance that he is considering, I ask about the large white unplugged refrigerator sitting in the middle of the garage.

"Isn't it great?" He's instantly gleeful as he opens the fridge door to reveal a clean, empty interior.

He found the fridge on Portland's Big Trash Day. Once a year, Portlanders empty their homes of old, damaged, and too-boring-to-live-with possessions, which they pile onto the sidewalk for the city to remove. For a week before BT Day, sidewalks all around Portland are encumbered by two-wheeled tricycles, twenty-year-old ranges, rickety shelf units, avocado kitchen cabinets, unsprung couches, seatless chairs, and rusted push mowers. While Public Works is supposed to take it all away, Portlanders recycle much of their neighbors' trash before the trucks and front loaders arrive. They take it home, clean it, repaint it, repair it — and if all else fails, set it out on the sidewalk the following year to be claimed by someone else.

On BT Day, Clarence rolled the fridge from the sidewalk into his garage. When he plugged it in, it whirred to life. So he blasted it clean with a borrowed power washer. "I think the owner just got tired of cleaning it," he says to explain the anomaly of a good refrigerator left out. Now he plans to get it to the basement and build a small storeroom around it.

"It will be a walk-in rose storage unit." He opens the door to reveal one shelf set low in the fridge to accommodate fifty eighteen-inch stems of hybrid tea. The extra cold storage will enable him to cut his exhibition roses as far ahead as the Wednesday before a Saturday show. "Big-time exhibitors own florist refrigerators. I think this is just as good."

Clarence loves to grow roses and he likes to exhibit them. His true passion, though, is making rose-related stuff. He's the founder of the Secondary Products Company, which he says is a "virtual reality company — no underlings — all benevolent bosses." He describes his company so convincingly that he's been known to fool the unwary. He was asked recently for a company catalog by a woman who wanted to order its products. In reality, the Secondary Products Company comprises three men: Clarence; John Mattia of Connecticut, who is an exhibitor and a digital rose artist; and Frank Benardella of New Jersey, a well-known independent breeder of miniature roses. The three men, plus "some other guys who like to travel around with us," invent rose-related uses for nonrose products, such as turning an old refrigerator into a storage unit.

In addition to rolling rose planters and rose refrigerators, Clarence has invented rose carriers made from polyvinyl chloride tubes wedged inside cut-down two-liter soda bottles set into the same kind of plastic bottle carriers that delivery trucks use. Add a handle made from more PVC tube and you have a Secondary Products Company portable rose transportation device.

"Where did you get the bottle carriers?"

"I went down to the Coke distributor, showed them what I'd done, and they gave me cases of them." He sounds delighted with their generosity, then adds, "Not bad, when you think about it, having a bunch of people walking through the exhibition carrying prize-winning 'Coca-Cola Roses.'"

He has turned freezer paper, plastic cups, and empty soda bottles into unspillable storage containers that hold fifty roses upright on a refrigerator shelf. He has soldered a long copper tube to a thumb-control spigot to create a one-of-a-kind extra long wand that squirts up, allowing him to spray the undersides of leaves without getting stabbed by thorns. He has also improved the design of a rose-bloom protector made from empty two-liter plastic juice bottles.

To make them, he cuts off the bottom of a bottle and wires it into position like a hat over the uncapped top; then he glues a clamp to the bottle's base. To use the bloom protector, you drive a pole into the soil near a flower that you want to protect, clamp the bloom protector to the pole and slide it into place over the flower. The hatlike top keeps moisture and ultraviolet light off the bloom, and the open bottom ensures air circulation.

"Wow," I say, impressed as much by the efforts of rose exhibitors to protect their treasures as by the ingenuity.

He nods. "These are nationally famous." Then he breaks the spell. "My biggest project right now is training sparrows to eat Japanese beetles right off my roses."

When I burst out laughing, Clarence grins in approval. "Lots of rose people are too serious. You have to have fun."

What makes it funnier is that he is serious.

As does anyone who has ever grown a rose, Clarence hates rose-destroying Japanese beetles, which swarm periodically despite the Diazanon that he sprays each year. He hates them so much that when he finds them on his plants, he picks them off and squishes them between his fingers "to get even." One day last year, Clarence noticed that sparrows appeared to be eating something off the grass where he had dropped dead beetles. The next day, he scattered squished beetles on a platform that he erected near the roses. Sure enough, the sparrows flocked to the platform for their feast. Next step was to find out if they would eat dead beetles from the rose plants.

"The problem is that sparrows don't hover. They need a perch."

He built them one. He shoved a long pole into the soil near a rose plant, attached quarter-inch, plastic-coated wire to the top of the pole and bent the wire around a rose cane to create a perch. He seeded the leaves of the rose with squished beetles and re-treated to his kitchen window to wait. The sparrows found their snack within a day.

In the driveway, surrounded by a head-high froth of burgundy, gold and cotton candy pink, Clarence demonstrates the flexible strength of the wire sparrow perch. He glances in my direction. His eyes sparkle. Next year, he'll let a mini – beetle infestation take hold in a corner of his garden and set up lots of perches. He plans to discover whether the sparrows will gobble up live beetles as hungrily as they do squished ones.

2

Crazy Rose People

 "You know Clarence?" John Mattia's tone is flat as he reconfirms my bona fides.

"Yes." I blurt without thinking, "I love Clarence."

Mattia doesn't hesitate. "I love Clarence, too. When I grow up, I want to be Clarence Rhodes."

We're standing in the front foyer of John's house in Orange, Connecticut. Crystal bowls and vases, porcelain plates, oak and silver engraved plaques sparkle on shelves in front of us. Since meeting Clarence, I have become fascinated by the exhibitors who will battle each other at the upcoming Spring National.

John has short gray hair, big aviator glasses, and the small, trim build and controlled-but-bouncy walk of an athlete. He began his career as a sportswriter and finished it as director emeritus of Public Affairs for Southern Connecticut State University. John speaks with the deadpan delivery of a stand-up comedian, except that he never plays for laughs. He is serious about work, family, friends, and roses.

Many of us grow the newest modern roses because we love their vibrant colors and nonstop bloom. Others of us plant old-garden roses, those created before 1867, because we love their history and sweet perfume. It's easy to appreciate why we would plant a flower for its carmine petals or honeyed scent and not hard to understand the appeal of heritage — planting an alba 'White Rose of York' beside gallica 'Red Rose of Lancaster'. But what about Clarence's nationally famous bloom protector? Or John's prize plaques? While millions of Americans pay obeisance to their roses by digging, watering, deadheading, and spraying, the country's several thousand exhibitors have been lured into a unique liaison with this ancient temptress. They labor for their plants more assiduously than the rest of us do; in return, they are allowed to hold beauty and shape its perfection. For the brief, heady hours of a rose show, they are in control of nature's most temperamental queen.

John Mattia doesn't seem like a man who craves power, but within moments of meeting him it is clear that he is enthralled by the hybrid teas that tint his backyard. When he speaks of them, his abrupt tone softens and his hands cup unconsciously around an invisible blossom.

"I have 225 rose plants in my yard and I know every one of them by name. They are as different from each other as people are. I holler at them sometimes. And I talk to them nicely. They know that my greatest joy has been to get out in the garden with them."

Like Clarence, John grows only hybrid teas. Unlike Clarence, John maintains a list of the names and characteristics of each variety, or named rose, in his garden. He plants varieties that win competitions and, in an impressive display of discipline, discards varieties — even beautiful ones — with which he doesn't win. (He generally gives them away to people who don't exhibit.)

Some exhibitors grow roses purely in order to compete. Yes, that means that if there were no rose shows, those exhibitors would not grow roses. The vast majority of exhibitors, though, including John, would grow roses no matter what. Competitions just offer another outlet for their obsession.

John's obsession started in 1965, when he and his wife, Gerry, moved into a new split-level ranch house on a curving street in Orange. John's brother Jim gave them two hybrid teas as a housewarming present. Not that Jim cared about roses, but Jim's neighbor, who owned a home-and-garden store, gave whatever plants he couldn't sell to his neighbors.

The Mattias were city people. John says that he can grow a tomato plant between sidewalk cracks, but he didn't know anything about decorative plants. He planted his brother's gift in the shade under a tree, the worst location he could have chosen for a sun-loving flower. "One died right away," he says. "I forgot about the other one."

A year passed. While shaving one morning the following August, he looked out the bathroom window and saw a little glow of yellow beneath the tree. His face still covered in white foam, he ran out to look. In that moment, his life changed. "It was the most beautiful thing you have ever seen."

The flower that had survived his inexperienced ministrations was one of the world's best-loved roses, a hybrid tea named 'Peace', whose conception is stuff of legend. The most romantic version of the story is that on the eve of World War II, French hybridizer François Meilland found a hybrid tea with large yellow-pink blossoms in his fields. He knew that he had something special, so he cut stems from the rose and got them into the American diplomatic pouch on the last plane to leave Paris before the Germans entered. The real story is that Meilland hedged his bets by also sending cuttings to Italy and Germany. At the end of the war, he discovered that the rose was a success in all three countries. The

Italians named it 'Gioia', or Joy; the Germans called it 'Gloria Dei', or Glory of God; and the Americans named it 'Peace'. Although its perfume is mild, its form is classic and its petals are the color of a pastel sunrise. 'Peace' is still widely available and well worth growing.

John cut the first blossom from his own 'Peace' for Gerry, who set it in front of a mirror to create the illusion of two flowers. Then, because this is what seems to happen to the susceptible, he read every book he could find on growing roses. And he started to dig.

The Mattias' backyard has direct southern exposure, which is ideal for a rose garden. The greensward that he had once described as "arguably the best lawn in Orange" disappeared in favor of raised beds colored with roses. Other flowers did not and still do not interest him. "If it isn't a rose, it's a weed," he says with a smile, but he's not joking.

Growing roses might have been enough for John had curiosity not drawn him to a rose show in Boston in 1977. One look at the top prize winners convinced him that he could do as well. A year later, he won the Novice Trophy at the New England Rose Show with a blossom from his 'Peace'. He grew that particular plant of 'Peace' for over thirty years. "What a survivor she was." As do most exhibitors, John loves — no, he adores — the urnlike shape of hybrid teas such as 'Peace'.

THAT FORM IS THOUSANDS of years removed from the simple six-petal flower pictured on the Minoan fresco of 1500 BCE. By about AD 1300 accidental and purposeful cross-breeding had produced many types of roses. Scholars and geneticists debate the origins and identity of these, but centifolia, damask, and gallica

are mentioned most often as being the earliest domesticated species grown in Europe and Asia Minor. Some historians add the
musk rose, or *Rosa moschata,* to this list; others demand the in-
clusion of the white rose, known as *R. alba.* Suffice to say that the
history of rose breeding is full of fascination and argument.

The origin of *R. gallica* may never be unequivocally determined,
but it seems to have flowered first in Persia before 1300 BCE and
traveled with successive waves of invading armies throughout the
then-known world. It's a low-growing, tough shrub that produces
brick red, seed-filled hips and fragrant crimson flowers that are
an essential ingredient in perfumes. By the seventeenth century,
gallica roses were the most popular class of cultivated rose with
over one thousand named varieties. One of the varieties, *R. gallica*
var. *officinalis,* the 'Apothecary's Rose', traveled to America with
the Puritans. It has fragrant double flowers. One hopes that it
gave the strict Puritans a few heady moments. It certainly spread
well in the New World and can be found suckering freely along
roadsides throughout the United States.

R. damascena, or the damask rose, is thought to have reached
the West from Syria by way of Egypt and Greece around 700
BCE. This is the rose whose 'Kazanlik' variety scents our modern perfumes. Its intense fragrance ensured its popularity, but it
was the damask's habit of blooming twice during a long growing
season that made it a star. The rose reached western Europe in the
saddlebags of returning Crusaders in 1187. (In his 1958 *History of
the Rose,* Roy Shepherd reports that the Crusaders left behind
enough roses to create five hundred camel loads of rose water
with which Saladin purified the Mosque of Omar after it had
been used as a Christian church.) By the eighteenth century the
French were growing a variation named 'Rose des Quatre Saisons'

(Rose of Four Seasons), whose name was an early example of false marketing. The rose bloomed twice, after all, not four times.

R. *centifolia,* also called the 'Cabbage Rose' for its multitude of overlapping petals, looks as most people imagine an old-garden rose, or OGR, should. It is pale pink or blush white and possesses a distinct rose scent. Herodotus may have given us our first sight of it in 410 BCE when he wrote, "In the gardens of Midas there grew roses that were so sweet that no others can vie with them and their blossoms have as many as 60 petals apiece." A few hundred years later, roses with over one hundred petals were described by Pliny. By the twelfth century, R. *centifolia* reached western Europe and Britain where Chaucer and Shakespeare celebrated it and Dutch masters loved to paint it.

In 1781 everything changed in the Western world when a rose found in China, R. *chinensis,* was planted in the Botanic Garden at Haarlem, Holland. It had pale pink, graceful blossoms held aloft on tall stems. The blooms did not have much fragrance and the plant sometimes froze to the ground during a tough winter. But it did what no other rose in the West did — it bloomed continuously throughout the growing season. Hybridizers immediately began to cross it with tougher roses in an attempt to create a hardy version.

The West still lacked a reliable yellow rose, but that changed in 1824, when Englishman John Damper Parks spotted a tea rose (R. *odorata*) with yellow flowers in the East India Tea Company gardens near Canton, China. Tea roses, by the way, possess their name because the blossoms smell faintly of crushed fresh tea leaves. The yellow tea rose proved to be an excellent parent. Soon the offspring of R. *chinensis* coupled with R. *odorata* were flowering across Europe and America. New rose variations appeared throughout the nineteenth and twentieth centuries — bourbons, boursaults, noisettes, polyanthas, hybrid perpetuals, and hybrid chinas. Each new type increased demand. When Sir Henry Willock returned from Iran in 1837 with a multipetal, deep yellow rose, demand skyrocketed. *R. foetida* var. *persiana* (Persian yellow rose) allowed breeders to create roses with vibrant yellow and orange shades that had never before been seen.

THE RESULTING PEACOCK colors have lured many gardeners over the years, but they don't tempt John. "Color is secondary." He shrugs. "Most people like the fragrance. Myself, I rarely smell them." He pauses, gently biting his lower lip, as if swayed by color and scent. Then, with a shake of the head, he says, "My interest is form."

John's formula for a perfect rose is: $\Delta + O + o$. The triangle shape represents the side view of a hybrid tea blossom. Like a triangle, the ideal bloom should have a wide flat base and the petals should bend inward slightly, rising to a high center. If you look down at the rose, all the outer petals should overlap in a concentric circle forming a large O. At the top is a tiny, fine center that forms a perfect little o. That is the hybrid tea shape that wins Queen — the best. Thus, $\Delta + O + o = Q$. To paraphrase Clarence Rhodes, this formula is nationally famous.

At a rose show, exhibitors may enter their blooms in many separate competitions, which are known as classes. Classes at a typical show include everything from the horticultural competitions such as One Hybrid Tea or Grandiflora Bloom without Side Buds or One Miniature or Mini-flora Bloom without Side Buds to arrangement contests, such as Rose Exhibited in a Picture Frame.

Most competitors exhibit modern roses. Although this category officially includes any variety created since 1867, most of the modern hybrid tea, floribunda, grandiflora, and miniature varieties presented at shows have been bred since 1970. Floribunda plants resemble hybrid teas, although they produce more flowers on each stem; they also tolerate more neglect than hybrid teas. Grandifloras also look a lot like hydrid teas, but their blooms are larger. Some rose lovers doubt that grandifloras are a true separate species. "It's a nebulous category," says John's friend Donna Fuss, who oversees America's oldest municipal rose garden in Connecticut's Elizabeth Park and also helped found the Connecticut Rose Society. "I think that breeders say, 'We haven't had a grandiflora in a long time; let's just say that this is one!'"

Some gardeners do exhibit old-garden roses that were hybridized before 1867. Yet no more than six of the often seventy-five classes in a show are devoted to OGRs, and only a hybrid tea is eligible to win Queen.

Judges award blue, red, or white ribbons to entries within each class; the best of the blue ribbon winners receives a trophy. Although Queen is the top award, there is no way to nominate your best bloom for the honor. Rose shows do not have a specific class designated "Queen." Instead, after all the flowers in a show have been judged, the blue-ribbon winners from the class One Hybrid Tea or Grandiflora Bloom are collected together and reevaluated by the judges. One of them is selected as Queen. King, Princess, and Best in Show are also chosen from this class. Similarly, only blossoms entered in the One Miniature or Mini-Flora Bloom class are eligible to win Miniature Queen, Miniature King, and Miniature Princess. It's from these two classes as well that judges select the twelve additional blooms that make up Court of Honor and Miniature Court of Honor.

John is a judge as well as exhibitor, but he loves most of all to exhibit. He has twice won Queen at ARS Nationals. He has twice won two of the next-place awards, King and Princess, at Nationals. In 2000 he took blooms to Montreal and won Queen at the Canadian National Rose Show. He has also won seven ARS National Challenge Class trophies, for which exhibitors enter a group of blossoms that meet specific criteria. These are the most coveted trophies other than Queen, because they are difficult and fiercely competitive. To win one is to make it in the exhibiting world, much as winning a major means success for professional golfers.

The Earl of Warwick Trophy, which John won at the Fall National in 2002, requires perfect specimens of six different varieties of hybrid tea, each of which must be on the All-America Rose Selections' roster of excellent roses. The blooms must be exhibited in separate vases and correctly labeled. Described like that, it sounds easy. But the test is to display perfect examples of six different varieties that look beautiful when set beside each other. Oh yes, your blooms must also be more beautiful and more perfect than your competitors' selections. The opportunities for failure abound, including curiously enough, labeling blooms correctly amid the heat of competition.

At first, the list of apparently petty requirements constituting a challenge class competition such as the Earl of Warwick seems extreme — six different All-Americas, perfect blooms, separate containers, legible labels, harmonious colors, and so on. It's daunting, and frankly, as the list of demands lengthens, a tad ridiculous. Why bother? In part, because challenge class competition provides a more complex chance to shape nature's beauty than a One Hybrid Tea or Grandiflora Bloom class. Also, fulfilling each challenge class requirement offers a chance to display proficiency. In lives that are rife with situations beyond our control, such as missing a child's soccer practice owing to an intransigent boss, it's satisfying to get all the steps right. Only one exhibitor can win the trophy, but all exhibitors who stage a challenge competition without forgetting something know that, in this instance at least, they didn't mess up.

Such moments contrast poignantly with all the times when you do mess up. John has never mislabeled a rose for a challenge trophy, but he has forgotten to put his own name on an entry tag, which he describes as his "biggest stupid mistake at a rose show." At the 1997 Spring National in Minneapolis, he entered the Herb Swim Trophy, which requires five different varieties of hybrid tea, one bloom per stem, each exhibited in a separate container. At the last minute, John switched some of the varieties in his entry and in the final seconds before the show closed, he rushed to fill out new entry tags for the substituted flowers. He got the right rose names on the right tags, but he forgot his own name. The judges later told him that but for the missing name on one tag, his entry was the winner. "Hands-down," John quotes the judges. Instead, his entry for the Herb Swim National Challenge Class Trophy was disqualified.

So why spend a fretful season tending your roses and three tense days cutting stems from them, in order to rise at 1 a.m. on a Saturday morning, pack the carrying crates, drive or fly too far, prepare or "groom" the blooms for four or five or six or even seven hours in a frigid hall, so that you can probably lose to someone with better blooms or someone who marks their tags correctly?

When I ask, John shifts on his toes like a boxer, bounce-bounce, beside the case in his foyer that is full of the dust-free crystal vases and porcelain plates won during twenty-seven years of competition.

"Because you might win. And even if you don't, it is sure fun trying." He runs a hand along the case of awards and his solemn face breaks into a grin. "Rose shows are the type of competition where even though I'm usually successful, I have as much fun not winning as I do winning. It's the participation. Win, lose, or draw, it's not the end of the world."

I must look doubtful, because he adds, "Well . . . mostly. When my roses have been kind to me, I have fun." He bounce-bounces again, impatiently. "Listen, exhibiting roses changed my life." His right thumb pops up. "Number one is the people I've met. I've got friends from all over the world. I may sound prejudiced when I say this, but there aren't any better people than rose people." Said with a finality that brooks no argument. His index finger follows the thumb. "Number two, exhibiting has taken me all over the country. There isn't a section of rose-growing America I have not been. Just last year, I went to Phoenix, Nashville, Chicago, and Washington, DC. I've been to Canada. Roses took me there. I tell you, I never got out of Connecticut until I got into roses."

John's passion for roses has taken him far beyond the venue of ARS competitions. As do many rosarians, he takes copious photographs of his favorite flower. During his first thirty-three years in roses, he shot four thousand slides; then, in 2001 Gerry gave John a digital camera for Christmas. In the following twenty-eight months, he shot 10,196 images of roses. He bought a professional-level camera, took a Photoshop course, installed a supersized printer.

"Now I've moved from taking rose photographs to having the rose tell a story." He superimposes images of roses onto other images that he has shot — fireworks explode across the climber 'Fourth of July'; a white dove rises from 'Peace'. "Every one of my pictures starts with a perfectly formed rose and evolves into something more."

John sells his digital photographs online. They've become a second career. "See what I mean? Roses changed my life."

But he has not abandoned rose shows. He was in Massachusetts when he committed his "second most stupid rose show mistake."

"It was 1979, the year after I won the Novice Trophy. At the time, I carried my roses in a soda case filled with empty Pepsi bottles. Not Coke bottles; Pepsi bottles, because I drank Pepsi. I'd put one rose in each Pepsi bottle, fill the bottle with water, put it in the case and put the whole thing in my trunk. I wanted to make the stems as long as possible, because I knew that all the best exhibitors won with roses that had the longest stems. So that year for the New England Rose Show, I cut sixty, maybe seventy, roses as long as possible, put them in the Pepsi bottles, put the bottles in the trunk, closed the trunk, and at 4 a.m., drove from New Haven to Boston to meet my friends Donna and Mike Fuss."

At 6:30 a.m., in a parking lot behind the exhibition hall, John opened the trunk and saw that the tops of his roses were smashed. He had cut the stems just a little bit too long. Encouraged by Donna and Mike, he managed to salvage enough "shorties" to enter the show and win a few ribbons. No trophies, though. Instead, he went home and built the first of many permutations of his rose transportation box.

"You want to see it?" He beckons me into the back hall toward the stairs, while making me promise to say nothing about the state of the basement, which turns out to be warm, dry, and only mildly cluttered.

After flicking on a light, John hands me an empty plastic gallon juice bottle from which the bottom has been removed and wired above the spout like a cap.

"Do you know what this is?"

"Oh, I do!" I feel absurdly proud of myself. "It's a bloom protector." John's eyebrows rise with surprise. I add, "Remember, I've been with Clarence."

"Of course. Well, I gave the idea to Clarence."

"He didn't tell me that."

John nods. "But I'll tell you where I got the idea. This is what I mean about rose exhibitors. When you play the game you are rivals, but you always share information. I was at the St. Louis convention in 1996, when Dennis Bridges from North Carolina said that he had to show me this ingenious new bloom protector. He'd gotten the idea from two other North Carolina exhibitors called the Wright Brothers — Fred and Jack Wright. I thought it was fantastic, so I came home and made two. Trouble is that Gerry and I can't drink that much juice. Then I found out that Clarence has a secret source for the bottles; so he makes them.

"Couple of years after St. Louis, I exhibited at a regional rose show down in Charlotte, North Carolina. It was really too late in the year for me to exhibit, but I won a trophy because of these babies. The morning that I cut the roses a frost covered the protectors, but the blooms inside were perfect. When I got up to accept the award, I thanked Fred and Jack Wright and Dennis and Suzy Bridges. Couldn't have done it without them." He holds the clear plastic contraption up to the light. "I have 109 of these babies thanks to Clarence."

CLARENCE, JOHN, FRED, JACK ... It's about now, in a basement full of rose paraphernalia, that I notice they're all men. The
only women have been escorted — Suzy by Dennis, Donna by
Mike. It reminds me of a long-ago visit to the men-only University Club in New York. My escort, a retired college president, kept
close hold of my right arm as he guided me toward the single room
that I could enter — a pink and gold "ladies luncheon room."

Come to think of it, during my historical research on roses,
the only women mentioned were Cleopatra and the empress
Josephine. I don't count Sappho, as we don't know if she did anything other than write about roses. Evidently, Cleopatra filled
her fountains with rose water and carpeted her bed and boudoir
with rose petals to attract that cad Marc Antony. It was heady
but ultimately ineffective. Josephine, though, managed to charm
Napoleon and build a garden that bloomed with all of the then-
known species and varieties of rose. At her estate, Malmaison, she
had 167 gallicas, twenty-seven centifolias, twenty-two chinas —
and the list continues. She even grew two American species. *R.
Carolina,* also called pasture rose, is a hardy, spreading plant
scented with deep pink, single blooms; the pink and white petals
of *R. setigera,* or prairie rose, flutter around large, egg-yolk yellow stamens. Some like the scent, others find it sickly sweet. Both
varieties were probably sent to Josephine by French missionaries
in Canada.

Josephine may have been one of very few famous women in
roses, but she deserves the highest of praise. Her delight in the
plant saved many species from extinction. Even her country's en-
emies esteemed her passion. When British ships seized French
vessels during the Napoleonic Wars, all botanical packages addressed to Malmaison were forwarded without incident. When

British troops entered Paris in 1815, they were commanded to protect the Malmaison collection.

It is believed that Malmaison's chief horticulturalist, André Dupont, was the first person to breed new varieties using artificial pollination. Josephine's patronage fueled his work and that of many other French hybridizers, who became masters of the profession. A 1791 catalog from a French grower listed only 25 rose varieties; by 1829 a similar catalog included 2,562.

Despite Cleopatra and Josephine, the world of roses is dominated by men. Many rose society members, and most exhibitors, hybridizers, and rose garden designers are men. In large part it's a legacy of traditional gender roles — women work inside; men work outside. Until recently, even the most rose-loving woman has been unlikely to become a professional gardener. As most designers and hybridizers began their careers as nurserymen who shoveled manure and planted vegetable marrows, those fields became effectively closed to women. Women were even less likely to become plant collectors, those swashbucklers of the eighteenth- and nineteenth-century plant world, who roved the globe looking for new and exotic species.

One of the most famous, Robert Fortune, took pistols and a fowling piece on his first horticultural hunting trip, which is fortunate, as he was attacked by robbers and pirates along the way. He also carried a Mandarin dictionary and spade — prudent for a Scotsman hunting plants in China.

Born in Edrom, Scotland, in 1812, Fortune left school after the primary grades to apprentice as a gardener. He showed immediate aptitude, and by 1840 he found a job at the Royal Botanic Gardens in Edinburgh. In 1842 he secured the position of superintendent of the Hothouse Department at the British Horticultural

Society. Yet the taciturn Scotsman possessed wanderlust as well as horticultural talent; he soon applied for the society's new position of collector in China. He got the job, for which lovers of roses, azaleas, bonsai, and tea should be eternally grateful.

Fortune spent most of the next nineteen years in China and Japan, searching for plants amid high adventure. On his first three-year trip, he survived typhoons in the Yellow Sea, pirates on the Yangtze River — that's where the fowling piece, aka double-barreled shotgun came in handy — and angry mobs in the northern provinces. The Opium Wars had just ended, and Westerners were unwelcome. He resorted to wearing local dress and shaving his head of all but the traditional pigtail; his Mandarin became proficient enough that he could pass himself off as Chinese, albeit always one "from a distant province." His disguise was so effective that he entered the Forbidden City of Souchow unchallenged.

Fortune wrote about his six expeditions in four best-selling books, which remain in print today. The thousands of plants that he discovered and shipped west on those trips in Dr. Nathaniel Ward's new invention, enclosed glass terrariums called Wardian cases, would be impossible to list here. But he is known to have encountered the plant now known as 'Fortune's Double Yellow' in the garden of a wealthy Mandarin in Ningpo. "On entering one of the gardens on a fine morning in May, I was struck by a mass of yellow flowers . . . I immediately ran up to the place, and to my surprise and delight found that I had discovered a most beautiful yellow climbing rose."

Not all of Fortune's travels were devoted to botanical discovery. On his second trip to China, paid by the East India Company, he disguised himself as a peasant and spirited twenty thousand tea plants and seedlings over the Himalayas to India, thereby establishing the Indian tea industry.

Fortune and his fellow horticultural adventurers left their wives at home as they wandered the known world. Plants, including roses, were a man's business. Even today, most of those with Donna Fuss's job — manager of a public rose garden — are men. In fact, Donna almost didn't get her post, despite being an ARS consulting rosarian and helping to save the garden from death by bulldozing during the 1970s. "They were nervous about giving it to me. A woman in the rose garden — nope, they didn't think that they could handle that. It was 1987, but there were still bastions of male power and the rose garden was one of them."

Yes, she says, roses are still very much a man's flower. "I think that's because they're so damn much work."

And that may be the truth of it. Until recently, roses were bulky, thorny objects that required a lot of strength to move and specialized equipment to control. The advent of disease-resistant miniatures that can grow in containers and carefree landscape varieties that thrive without much pruning may lure more women to the Queen of Flowers. A woman even served a recent term as ARS president. Marilyn Wellen is only the second female elected to that position in the organization's 108-year history. The times, they may be a-changing.

FOR THE MOMENT, THOUGH, I squat down beside John to examine his rose transportation box, which resembles a Pullman traveling case of yesteryear. Instead of wool suits and Fedora hats, each box holds eighteen cut roses with twenty-one-inch stems. The boxes are lined with dense foam and wooden racks into which the roses fit. To load a box, John pushes the stem of each rose into a glass tube designed to root Cymbidium orchids. He likes the size of these tubes and the distinct lip around the opening that holds fast to the medical film with which he seals them after filling them with water. He lays the filled sealed tubes of roses flat across the rack, alternating blossom and stem ends. Over this rack, he fits a wood-and-string frame filled with four cold packs to keep the roses from opening into full bloom too quickly. (John made the mistake of using chicken wire rather than string in an earlier version of the cold frame. As the water vapor in the box condensed, it dripped from the metal chicken wire and spotted the blooms below.) Finally, he screws the cover into place. Once sealed, John guarantees that the boxes can be turned upside down without affecting the roses.

"I'll never forget St. Louis in '96. That was the first time I used these. I'm walking along to pick up my luggage at the airport and about a hundred yards away from the luggage carousel, I see bags flying up into the air like a volcano before slamming back down onto the belt. I start running down the hall, shouting, 'Stop! Stop! You can't put my baggage onto the conveyor like that!' Just as I arrive, my two big boxes come soaring out. I thought, 'Oh, no.' But when I opened the boxes, I found that I'd only lost one rose out of thirty-six. I had three roses in the Court of Honor that year, plus King and Princess." John pats the box beside us with satisfaction.

That's when I notice that he is demonstrating equipment instead of showing off flowers. He's an accomplished rosarian and expert exhibitor. His digital rose art sells well, and his straight-ahead rose photographs often grace the cover of the ARS magazine *American Rose*. But right now he reminds me of a weekend grill-meister who cares more for his barbecue tools than for the steak he's supposed to cook. I reexamine the transportation box and the bloom protectors; I think of Clarence's sparrow perches and the weighted ropes that were cut to fall precisely over the winter rose tunnels. They remind me that whether it's a five-speed lawn tractor or a fifteen-blade Swiss Army knife, guys love gear. It's not just her heady scent, tantalizing colors, and sexy form; men are fascinated by the Queen of Flowers because they need so much stuff in order to manage her.

As if to demonstrate my point, John drops to his haunches beside a battered blue metal box.

"Fishing tackle box?" I hazard. John shakes his head as he lifts the lid, revealing two trays filled with a scattering of small metal tools and an assortment of incongruous items, including what looks like a turkey baster.

"Toolbox." A toolbox full of items that an exhibitor needs to groom roses into perfection in the predawn hours before a show. He picks out an item to show me. "Turkey baster for topping off the vases with water."

The box also holds nail scissors to trim uneven petals; small green foam wedges that are used to hold floppy stems upright in vases; deckle-edged scissors to realistically trim leaves whose edges are brown; a shoe mitt to buff the leaves; nail clippers to remove thorns; cosmetic brushes whose narrow handles are used to arrange petals into the required spiral; Q-tips that when inserted between tight rose-petals gentle them apart; rubber bands because "you never know" — what you never know, I'm not sure; and sheets of hot-pink stickies on which John writes the names of the varieties he is showing.

The box represents what John most loves about his favorite

flower. "Grooming roses is more interesting for me than growing roses. See, I've always loved symmetry. That's what you're looking for when you groom a rose. You move petals to fill in the voids and to make the roses symmetrical. Of course, you have to grow them right to begin with. You can't take a bad rose and make it a Queen. They say you can, but you cannot. The rose has to have potential."

Donna Fuss says that exhibitors who groom well are artists. Rather like portrait photographers, they are able to transform an attractive bloom into the image of perfection. "It's a gift," she explains. "Many of us who belong to rose societies can grow beautiful garden flowers — that's our goal. But an exhibitor like John can look at a blossom and know exactly what he needs to do to achieve a certain look. You either have that skill, or you don't."

Since we've been talking about male fascination with the rose, Donna's comments make me think of male fashion designers and hair stylists who specialize in making women look beautiful. They coddle and compliment; disguise wide hips with ingenious draping; and find the perfect cut for frizzy locks. Such men serve women, yet they also guide them. By buying this dress or that haircut, we accept their image of us. Just as a hybrid tea takes on the appearance that John Mattia wishes it to, women look the way men with scissors see us. In each case, though, the females have thorns, which may be part of the infatuation. Dangerous women have tempted men since Eve handed Adam an apple.

Speaking of tools, the bottom shelf of John's grooming box also holds a screwdriver. "This is the most important item in here. I use it to open the rose box. You want a good rose story? When I got to St. Louis in '96, after the volcano that nearly wiped out my rose boxes, I get to the hotel and find that I've forgotten my screwdriver. It's ten o'clock at night. All the stores in the neighborhood are closed. I have to start grooming at 4 a.m. I ask the hotel staff to try and find one for me. Meanwhile, I go get something to eat at a restaurant across the street from the hotel. Coming back, guess what was lying in the middle of the road?" He hefts the tool. "*This* screwdriver."

He stands up so suddenly and buoyantly that he seems to have springs in his legs.

"Show season." He makes it sound like the celebratory slap of a high five. "The Spring National's on May 8 in San Diego this year. I can't go, but you'll be fine. You're gonna meet Cal Hayes. Outstanding gardener. One of the best all-time exhibitors. Cal will be going for a new record — a sixth Nicholson Trophy. Jeff Stage. He's one of the best grooming teachers around. He's going to be given the ARS's highest service award, but he doesn't know it yet. If you meet him ahead of time . . . "

"I swear, not a word."

"Okay." John stands a moment in thought, then smiles. "Start with Rachel Hunter. She's a firecracker."

3

Hard Pruning

Rachel Hunter's run for the roses began during a high school typing competition when she was faced with a perfect classmate — one of those pretty, popular, brilliant students who drive the rest of us into self-conscious despair.

"I was a fast typist," says Rachel, drawing out the word fast like a car revving its engine. "The best typist in school had a chance to compete in the National Typing Competition, and I did not want this girl who had everything else in life to beat me." Rachel holds out her hands, fingers dancing on an imaginary typewriter. John's description of Rachel was perfect — from her cap of flame-colored hair to her scarlet toenails, Rachel is a firecracker. "If I have an aptitude for something, I go all out," she says.

Rachel practiced until her fingertips went numb. She beat the perfect girl and won the New England Regionals. But she came in third at the Nationals. "Third isn't a win," she says with a shrug. But it does mean that in 1964 Rachel Hunter was the third-fastest competitive typist in America.

Then she fell in love with a man who drove fast cars. In 1973 she and Phil Hunter drove a yellow Corvette to Las Vegas, got married in the Silver Bell Wedding Chapel, and saw Elvis Presley's midnight show.

"These days, you can be married by Elvis," jokes Phil, a tall, gentle man with a wide grin that lights his long face.

Rachel took to cars as she had taken to Phil. Throughout the early 1970s they raced a 1962 Plymouth and 1969 Dodge Dart at the Orange County, California, drag strip every chance they got.

"Before the light turns green, you have to be working your foot on the gas pedal." Rachel taps her right foot reminiscently.

"Rachel was quicker than I was," says Phil.

She nods. "I had real good reflexes then." She laughs — a bubbling sound that dances from low to high as she remembers. "It was very, very loud at the racetrack and very exciting. I loved the competition."

Her best time for a quarter-mile race in the 600-horsepower Dodge Dart was 123 mph in 11.10 seconds. By 1978, she and Phil realized that his career with UPS was a surer bet. They sold the cars. "Still hurts to think about it." Rachel's brow wrinkles.

In the 1980s she tried bowling, yet she could not maintain a high enough score to compete professionally. In 1987 Phil was transferred from Los Angeles to Louisville. That's where Rachel went all out for roses.

She had been growing roses ever since she and Phil bought their first house in Cerritos. She had started with five plants, including the perfumed red hybrid tea, 'Mr. Lincoln', which she still grows over thirty years later. Rachel and Phil moved three times in California, and with each relocation she increased the size of her garden — five plants became fifteen; fifteen grew to thirty-five. "I was still just growing and cutting, though. Making fragrant bouquets for the house. That's all."

The new house in Louisville sat on three-quarters of an acre. That was enough room for lots of roses. "But before we started planting, I said that I had to join a rose society to learn how to grow these babies where there is a winter." Rachel joined the Louisville Rose Society. "I figured that I'd stay in for one year, learn how to take care of my roses, and then I'll bail out."

Ah, best laid plans . . . Rachel had a friend who talked constantly about rose shows.

"I said, 'What's a rose show?'"

"'It's where everyone brings their roses, and you win awards and ribbons.'"

"Bla, bla, bla." Rachel grins. "I thought, 'Who cares?' But she kept after me, so in 1988, she and I went to the Louisville Rose Society Show and my jaw dropped. I thought that I grew roses pretty well, but when I saw those show winners, I knew that I wanted to do whatever those people were doing to their plants."

She did — aged horse manure, fertilizer, compost, lots of water. Pretty soon, she says, "I was getting great results."

That was when her enabling friend persuaded her to enter a few blooms in the Kentucky State Fair flower show.

"Right out of the chute I won Best Miniature Spray for a variety called 'Choo Choo Centennial'. Well, that was it; I was hooked. I've been exhibiting ever since." She sweeps an arm. "What do you think?"

Three hundred fifty hybrid teas, floribunda, and miniatures color bark-mulched beds set into a large stone patio. It sits on a rise above Rachel and Phil's sleekly modern home on ten acres above Temecula, California. Two stone swans, their necks entwined, rise above a splashing fountain in the center of the garden. At the far end, beside a small swath of emerald grass, an octagonal white gazebo offers welcome respite from the sun. This is Rachel and Phil's retirement dream home, custom built around a koi fish pond, whose gold, silver, and black and white inhabitants flash beneath a glass-floored walkway. Phil exhibits the koi, and they both grow roses for competition.

When couples compete together in rose shows, one member of the unit is almost always the boss. In this case it's Rachel. Phil is an avid gardener who has educated himself about roses. He likes them, and when asked he willingly helps prune, protect, and transport. In truth, though, he prefers the exotic protea and Australian banksia that he nurtures on a hill behind their home.

When both members of a couple are equally enamored, they must devise a way to work together as equals. It can be difficult; most of us have found cooperation to be hard ever since we were forced to share our favorite shovel in the sandbox. Louise Coleman, author of two articles for the ARS magazine, "How to Grow Roses Together and Stay Married" and "How to Exhibit Together and Stay Married," describes the problems. "I'd go to feed the roses and find out that my husband had fed the roses. He would spray and find out that I had already sprayed. I would order twenty roses and he would order twenty different roses. We never fought about money, kids, or sex. We fought about roses!"

She devised a rose-care system to save their marriage: He cared for the roses from the ground down, she from the ground up. He became the expert on soils, planting, and fertilizing. She sprayed, pruned, and timed the bloom cycle for the shows. It worked, she says. Without competition they could concentrate on each other and their shared passion for roses.

Right now, Rachel and Phil are sharing the pruning. Most gardeners prune their roses when they see signs of spring growth;

many of us do no more than tidy them up a bit for a season of flowers. In contrast, exhibitors hard-prune, or cut back, their plants
by at least one-third. Hybrid teas and miniatures bloom best on
new growth; hybrid teas, in particular, must be severely pruned
at the start of each growing season to produce long, strong canes
that support large blossoms. Exhibitors schedule their pruning
sessions to force plants into bloom for specific competitions. Timing is everything.

The spring show season in the southern California region begins in late April and runs into early June. Exhibitors who plan
to work the entire season of local shows and have enough blooms
for the Spring National on May 8 need their roses to be in peak
bloom throughout. To achieve this, they spread out their pruning
over four to six weeks. Staggering it permits the blossoms to open
over the course of the spring show season. Rachel and Phil began
on January 1. With sharpened red Felco pruners — all exhibitors seem to use Felcos — they headed into the section of garden
nearest the house. For the next thirty days, they worked through
the yard much as cotton pickers move across a field — bending,
cutting, tossing plant material. They hard-pruned about seventy
roses a week. It's now February 4; only a few hybrid teas are left
to cut. Rachel bends over a forty-five-inch-high plant labeled
'Gemini'.

"I love this rose," she says, her voice muffled by foliage. 'Gemini' was bred by Keith Zary of Jackson & Perkins. Its lightly fragrant pink and white blossoms often measure five inches across.
Rachel describes it as "a real show rose with perfect hybrid tea
form. But it's also a good garden rose; very disease resistant. Can't
say that for all of them!"

Holding the top of a fat green cane with one hand, she slices off almost twenty inches of growth, sets it aside, grasps and cuts another. She works quickly, her gloved hand squeezing the bypass pruners hard and fast — snick, snick — each cut angled forty-five degrees a half inch above a leaf axle from which a new flowering cane will grow. She shears the plant in twenty minutes, then straightens with a slight groan.

I, who inevitably emerge bloodied from forty-minute encounters with my own roses, am dazzled. "That angled cut takes me forever," I offer.

Rachel holds her left hand at her lower back. "The new thinking is that it doesn't matter. Cut straight across if you want." She shrugs. "But it's the way I learned; too late to change now."

Rachel *has* changed her habit of listening to music on earphones while she prunes. She stopped the day she found a rattlesnake wrapped around a floribunda. Evidently, rattlesnakes use the thorny canes to help them shed their skin. "Useful for *them*, but I want to be able to navigate my garden without fear! So no more earphones, because I might not hear the rattle."

"Actually, the babies that come out in April are the most dangerous." Phil smiles blandly. "Their rattle doesn't make a sound."

Even with my untrained eye, I can see that Rachel and Phil's staggered pruning has produced the desired result. The plants at one end of the garden are full of fat buds; those in the middle near the fountain have walnut-sized buds; the newly shorn plants around us have none. Rachel plants multiples of the same variety in each section of the garden to ensure that she always has at least one flowering representative of each type throughout the show season. Growing twelve of a variety rather than two gives Rachel a better chance of having a Queen-worthy pink and white blossom at the Spring National on May 8.

She groups them — three in one area, four in another — so that she can quickly see how well a particular variety grows over the season. Eleven other 'Gemini' are scattered this way throughout the beds. The visual result of her practical approach to winning is stunning. In full bloom the rose garden quilts the ground around the fountain in patches of raspberry, buff pink, coral, cream, lemon, and a burgundy so deep that it's almost black velvet.

The diversity of roses today is dazzling. While Rachel grows only three types — hybrid teas, floribundas, and miniatures — she can choose from a range of colors that leaves the brightest rainbow in the shade. Not content with single-color blooms, breeders create striped roses, bicolor blossoms, and blooms whose fuchsia base blends into yellow petals tipped with peach. Pastel or saturated, the blossoms can have five or sixty-five petals, which might be as translucent as a butterfly wing or as thick as the sturdiest eggshell. Flowers can be as narrow as a vase or as round as a teacup. Foliage can be shiny or dull. And the plant itself might be six inches or six feet high. I am beginning to understand why rosarians insist that the rose, in its multiplicity, can constitute an entire garden.

Rachel bends over one more plant and begins to prune, this time with a sigh. The metal label stuck into the mulch reads 'Brandenburg Gate'. When I look it up later, I discover that it's a 1991 Jackson & Perkins hybrid tea with big, bright red blossoms. "This did well for us in Kentucky, so we brought it with us when we moved. But it just doesn't look good here. Its form is just ewww." She makes a mewing sound and sticks out her tongue. "Same is true of 'Louise Estes'" — a fruity pink-blend Joseph Winchel hybrid tea.

When Rachel and Phil left Kentucky for their return to California, they took fifty full-grown roses with them. It was February, so the roses were dormant. Rachel dug them up and plopped them into five-gallon pots. "They were the first things we put onto the U-Haul truck. Then we put all our belongings behind the roses. At the California border when asked if we had any plants, fruits, or vegetables, I said, 'Just this apple I'm eating, officer!'" Rachel grins wickedly. "Oooh, I know. Illegal. But they were hard-to-find varieties! And I knew for sure that there wasn't a bug anywhere on them."

They timed their move carefully. February is the perfect rose-planting month in southern California. "The rose garden was the first thing to get established here; I made sure of that." Now, though, with results of the final pruning coloring the ground at her feet, she adds ruefully, "I wasted a lot of time moving and cultivating roses that were nice, strong show plants back there but turn out to be nothing out here."

It takes a couple of years to know whether a rose, or any plant, for that matter, will transplant well to radically different surroundings. But by the third or fourth year, as Rachel explains, "You should say, 'This is it.'" Decision time has been tough on her Kentucky-bred roses. She only has three 'Brandenburg Gate' left. "I got rid of two, but I love it so much. I keep hoping that it's going to do something!"

When she first started, Rachel was so gung-ho that she would only put a variety in the garden that would perform on the show table. If it didn't win in two years, out it would go. Now they might receive a year of reprieve.

"But during that year, you are always asking, 'Should I keep it or dump it? How much care does it need? Does it travel well to shows? Did it win? Did it win enough?'"

If it doesn't win enough, out it goes, but Rachel no longer replaces the losers with brand-new varieties. In Kentucky, she says, "When something new came out I wanted to be the first kid on the block to have it, because in the Midwest a new variety stood a good chance of winning Queen. But that tactic doesn't work with the judges in California."

"They will not give Queen to a new rose out here until they've seen it around for a year or so," explains Phil. "We were the first ones showing 'Brook's Red' and we didn't even get a blue ribbon the first times we exhibited it!"

Now they choose their new plants from each year's prize winners. They grow them for a few years in a protected test bed beside Phil's giant compost pile before permitting them into the main garden.

"That reminds me of parents who have a children's table and a grown-up table at Thanksgiving dinner," I say.

"Just about," Rachel laughs. "You gotta know if they can behave."

Right now, they are evaluating the manners of three hybrid teas — raspberry 'Ida', which also smells like a raspberry; red-and-white 'Stephanie Ann'; and apricot 'Sunstruck'.

Replacing ten plants a year at an average cost of fifteen to twenty dollars per plant is financially manageable for most gardeners, but many exhibitors buy twenty, thirty, even fifty new plants annually. Add up the cost of plants, chemicals, and equipment, and it is obvious that competition roses cost money. It's not the most expensive form of horticultural obsession — fancy orchids cost more than fancy roses — but the price tag is one reason why many exhibitors are well-paid doctors, lawyers, executives, and scientists.

The habit of thrift runs deep in the community, though. Rosarians routinely boast about the number of plants in their garden

that began as budwood instead of nursery stock. Budwood is a
four- to six-inch cutting from the cane, or stem, of a rose plant.
Rosarians the world over send each other plants this way. Dennis
Bridges, of the Bridges/Wright Bloom Protector, is known for
sharing budwood from the best specimen of his current favorite
rose with his competitors, because "you can't be a good competitor without good competitive stock."

In addition to sharing favorites, distributing budwood is an
inexpensive way to test the strengths and weaknesses of a newly
bred rose. ARS president Steve Jones has sent budwood of
'Dorothy Rose', an orange and white striped mini that he named
for his mother, to friends all over the country. So far, the plant
has proved resistant to rust, a fungal disease that plagues rose foliage with unsightly orange and yellow blotches. "Not sure how
hardy it is, though." Steve has sent it to friends in the North to
find out if it will survive their winters.

Most rosarians ship budwood wrapped in damp wadding
inside a paperboard container. John Mattia favors damp paper
towels and a resealable plastic bag inside a UPS three-day mailer.
Cigar-smoking Bob Martin, whose book *Showing Good Roses* is
the exhibitors' how-to bible, packs his budwood in wooden cigar
boxes. They provide his friends with a colorful keepsake even if
the cutting doesn't take. Much of his budwood does well, though;
lots of exhibitors grow three Martin-bred varieties: 'Pasadena
Star', 'Peachy Cheeks', and 'Bolivar' — the last named for the cigar box in which it arrived.

To produce a plant from budwood, rosarians graft it onto a
variety that consistently produces strong roots. To graft a rose,
Phil cuts a two-inch split down a healthy thick cane on 'Fortune-
ana' or 'Dr. Huey', slides the budwood into the split, and wraps

the join. Lots of rosarians wrap it with Parafilm, a flexible, self-sealing film used by scientists, doctors, and gardeners. Five inches below the graft, he cuts almost, but not quite through, the cane, and wraps this wound in sphagnum moss. Four months later, when the graft has grown together, the Parafilm has popped off, and roots protrude from the sphagnum moss, he cuts the cane just below the new roots, plants the baby rose in a pot, and sets the pot in a misting box. Two months later — six months after grafting — the new rose is set into the garden.

Phil points to a new cutting planted beneath shade cloth. " 'Polo Queen' from Cal Hayes." Cal is the exhibitor who John Mattia said will be trying for his sixth Nicholson Challenge Bowl at the National in San Diego. The Nicholson, which is the most coveted challenge class award, has been awarded at ARS Spring Nationals since 1925. Named for Englishman R. A. Nicholson, who donated the giant silver trophy, it requires nine hybrid tea blooms, each a different variety, exhibited in separate containers.

Cal grows 250 hybrid teas and two hundred miniatures in his Santa Ana garden, where he also experiments with hybridizing. In 2003 he discovered a pink sport on pink and white 'Cajun Moon' and named it 'Polo Queen' for his water polo–playing granddaughter. A sport is a differently colored blossom caused by a genetic mutation. Phil says that so far 'Polo Queen' is a winner — well formed, disease resistant, with repeat-blooming, exhibition-form blossoms.

In addition to budwood cuttings, most rosarians laud their homemade equipment. I never saw a purchased misting box, and everyone who owned a florist's refrigerator hastened to say that they'd bought it secondhand. Rachel and Phil's own refrigerator is a Sears chest-style freezer that Phil has modified with an exterior thermostat called a chiller controller. Plug the freezer into the controller and the controller into an outlet, set the desired temperature and voilà — a sixty-stem refrigerator that costs several hundred dollars instead of several thousand.

The unit doesn't lose heat as quickly as an upright. And Rachel likes being able to open the lid and look down on the blossoms, which she has been known to keep fresh successfully for as long as two weeks. "If a blossom has blown its center, it's easy to pull it up, throw it away, and make room for a new one." Her gold bracelets clink against each other as she reaches into the chest and mimes the movement of pulling and tossing.

I imagine her lifting the lid on a chest full of blossoms, being filled with their beauty as she checks their health. Ha — my romantic notions crack her up. Rachel allows herself to feel sentimental about certain plants in the rose garden, but she doesn't commune with the blooms in the chest. Their responsibility is to look great; her job is to cull the wimps and reward the beauties with a predawn trip to the show. She always culls and loads from right to left, so even if the blown rose came from the left side of the chest, the new one will go on the right. "That way I'm never confused at two in the morning about which roses are too old to compete." She taps her forehead with a pink polished fingernail.

As we peer into her freezer – cum – rose refrigerator, I realize that while Clarence's Secondary Products Company is imaginary, it's modeled on the actual practice of the majority of exhibitors. Freezers become fridges. Spare parts become misting boxes. Supplies are often purchased in supersized containers and shared among friends. Clean half-gallon milk cartons are the container of choice when transporting roses a few miles by car; exhibitors

traveling farther rely on Rubbermaid coolers and modified suit-
cases like John Mattia's. These habits mean that while doctors
abound on the ARS rolls, you don't have to be rich to be obsessed
with roses. Truck drivers, mechanics, teachers, ministers, super-
market managers, and social workers belong to rose societies,
grow first-class plants, and show prize-winning blossoms. Rosarians are proud of this inclusiveness. They often told me that rose
societies are the *only* places where brain surgeons and construction workers are social equals.

It also is true that rosarians are simply disinterested in one another's nonrose lives. Friendships abound, but when asked, many
rose buddies have only the vaguest idea of the neighborhood
in which their colleagues live, their employment status, or how
many children they have. They learn that someone has a romantic partner if that person appears at a meeting or show; otherwise
the topic many never arise. Only the roses matter. So whether or
not white-collar and blue-collar professionals interact seamlessly
in meetings, skill with roses may be the great social leveler that
their proponents profess it to be.

As we walk back to the garden, wind blows Rachel's copper hair about like a flame. "If it starts gusting real bad, all these
canes are going to be blowing into each other. They stab and tear
at each other. They tear the foliage right off." Her cheerful de-
meanor disappears in a frown of worry. The Spring National is
just six weeks away. "I work so hard on these babies. Then the
wind will come up, and in a few minutes it'll destroy everything.
It happens every spring up in these hills." She sighs. "Makes me
feel hopeless enough to give up. But I've promised Geri that if she
goes to the National, I will too."

Geri Minot McCarron coaches track and teaches high school English in San Diego. When she's not in school, she and her husband, Alan McCarron, raise three hundred roses and one horse named Samwise in the hills inland from San Diego. Horses are an interest that runs in the family: Alan's bother is Hall of Fame jockey Chris McCarron; Geri and Alan met at a racetrack, and they own several racehorses in partnership with friends. Geri says that Samwise loves roses as much as they do. He demonstrates his passion by eating any rose he gets close to, thorns and all. In addition to his drastic pruning method, he provides manure for the alfalfa tea that Geri pours over the plants. "It's the best rose potion ever, bar none." Samwise's used straw also provides a lot of mulch material.

Like Rachel, Geri first entered her roses into competition at a state fair. "It was such a thrill to carry a rose that I had grown into a public display; it was a living work of art that I had sculpted." After she and Alan fell in love, he began to show roses with her. "Men like to win," explains Geri, then adds, "Mainly, Alan likes to give flowers to everyone he knows. He has even used them to quiet crying babies near him in church; the flowers really get the youngsters' attention."

She and Alan still exhibit at fairs, as well as in ARS shows. While the fairs aren't as rigorous, "a few hundred thousand more people see the flowers there and it's fun to see our names up on the winner's table." The artist's reward and the pleasure in winning local fame has kept her laboring in the garden for fifteen years through wind, hail, snow, and drought. "I teach Greek mythology every fall, and it's a constant reminder that man is at the mercy of the forces of nature."

The lesson that nature is in charge is hard won for most gardeners. Yellow dandelions insist on sprouting in emerald lawns; squirrels rearrange daffodil bulbs; and a spring blizzard inevitably blasts through just before you can get out to cut the flowering branches of forsythia. Humility and an open mind may be our greatest assets in the yard. Several years ago, I moved thyme out of a gravel walkway into which it had crept and back to the garden bed where I wanted it three times before I stopped trying to wrest control. After all, thyme prefers full sun and unimproved rocky soil that drains fast, in other words, the gravel path. Still a little miffed, I planted creeping phlox subulata, or moss pink, in the abandoned border. When both it and the thyme flourished, I was grateful that I'd been forced to listen. And then, I must admit, I returned to persuading the intoxicatingly scented antique shrub 'Louise Odier' to grow in partial shade. She couldn't be convinced and finally died in frustration. These lessons, as I said, are hard won.

Geri compares showing roses to the track-and-field sports that she coaches. "There is a need in both for determination, physical endurance and a willingness to keep going even when the legs are tired." She has only been to a few ARS Nationals and has never won a big award. "Given the weather we've had, maybe I shouldn't bother to go to this one. But Rachel and I have promised each other that we're going to try our very hardest — 100 percent effort one last time. No one said this was supposed to be easy."

Exhibitors all said the same — show roses fascinate because they are difficult to cultivate. As one gardener told me, "You fight Father Time and Mother Nature, so you can never win."

In contrast, many of today's garden roses, such as the shrub 'Carefree Delight' and the floribunda 'Playboy', are easy to grow. Undemanding varieties are increasingly popular, which is good, say rosarians. The shrub 'Knockout' is the world's best-selling rose, in large part because anyone can grow it. "You don't have to do anything but stick it in the ground and water it," explains Claude Graves, a longtime ARS member who is enthusiastic about all roses. Easy varieties that offer fragrance and a painter's palette of colors keep the weekend gardener interested, and the more roses in people's yards, the better. As Claude says, why grow a "green mustache" of holly or juniper around your house, "when you can grow good shrub roses that will give you foliage and a beautiful flush of bloom."

In fact, the foliage can be beautiful as well. Before meeting Clarence, I thought that the leaves of most roses looked alike. I've since realized that they deviate significantly. Color ranges from dusty gray to Irish green; growth pattern may be the typical cluster of five leaflets, but it might also be the fernlike appearance created by fifteen leaflets; surfaces can be smooth or deeply ribbed; texture varies from velvet to waxy; some edges are smooth, some as serrated as a bread knife. And the scent — yes, scent. Some antique varieties, including *Rosa eglanteria* and *R. primula,* smell of apples or incense when bruised. Yet one more reason to replace those anonymous evergreens beneath your front windows with the Queen of Flowers.

While exhibitors applaud the availability of trouble-free plants for the average grass-growing American, they are not personally interested in something so straightforward. "But he who dares not grasp the thorn should never crave the rose," wrote English novelist Anne Brontë. Gardeners who survive their tough roses are seen as the true rosarians. Roses are not just a flowering shrub beside the lawn for them; they are an avocation. And avocations should engage the brain. As Cal Hayes says, "An easy hobby is a boring hobby."

I am reminded of my friend Robin whose spring garden blooms with thousands of crocus, daffodils and tulips; they paint the soil in pastel hues beneath flowering crabapples and epitomize spring's rebirth. Yet despite chairs positioned just so near a climbing wisteria, I have never seen Robin rest in her Eden. Instead, she weeds, prunes, plants, and plans. She is as absorbed by her tulip design as painters are by their composition. When complimented, she says quickly, "Yes, yes, it *is* wonderful, isn't it. But wait until you see what I intend for next year!"

At a time when the great American pastime has devolved into watching reality television shows, it is edifying to spend time with people who want to be challenged by their hobby. It offers a lesson in the energizing effect of effort.

Rachel may struggle with her finicky exhibition hybrid teas, but she says that she won't forsake them. "They're the classic. When I think of a rose, I think long stem, beautiful foliage, exquisite form. The hybrid tea has all of those qualities. Oh, I know that old-garden roses have been around a whole lot longer, but they don't hit my button."

While some rosarians, such as Claude Graves and Donna Fuss, grow both old-garden and modern roses, many exhibitors grow only one or the other. They form constituencies much like Democrats and Republicans. At their most extreme, OGR lovers won't grow anything hybridized after 1900. If you object that old roses bloom only once, OGR fanatics will say, "Yes, but such lovely red hips!" without mentioning that the hips may take six months to turn red. On the other hand, visual perfection is so important to some modern-rose proponents that they spray excessively and are liable to say that the only good bug is a dead bug. They consider old roses to be noxious weeds. Claude, who belongs to the Heritage Rose Foundation as well as the American Rose Society, describes each camp as "rose snobs."

"They think that their particular niche is the only niche, their ideas the only ideas." He met people with the same propensity when he joined Trout Unlimited years ago. "'Fishing snobs,' I call them. The folks who fished with dry flies didn't approve of people who used nymphs. The catch-and-releasers despised the catch-and-eaters. Seems like people just always want to choose up sides."

Rachel may love the look of hybrid teas, but her passion for exhibiting them is practical, she says, not snobbish.

"The Queen of Show is always a hybrid tea, so . . . " She shrugs. So the garden is planted in a breath-taking spot, but make no mistake — the pretty flowers are intended to bring victory. Wind or no wind, in six weeks, she'll be shooting for the Nicholson. "Yes, I know Cal's going for it again! But I'll try anyway. In all these years of exhibiting, I've never accomplished it. It's a goal, definitely a goal."

4

Rose Sex

 "I hated roses when I first came here. Did Keith tell you?" Debbie Vachuda whips a baby rose, roots flailing, from potting soil and drops it into a four-foot-high plastic garbage can. "Hated them." She uproots a pink-budded one. "But Keith converted me. I'm madly in love with roses now." She lets go. The seedling plummets into the trash.

Deeply tanned and lanky in blue jeans, Dr. Keith Zary leans against another planting bench as he watches his assistant kill roses.

"Debbie has a cold heart. That's why she's so good." Debbie laughs. Keith smiles.

"Shove this up your nose." Debbie decapitates an apricot seedling and holds the blossom toward us.

Keith leans over to inhale. "Nice."

I sniff. "Oh, that's lovely." It actually smells of apricots.

Debbie drops blossom and seedling onto a rising mound of sacrifices in the trash barrel. "Slow grower, sparse bloom, poor form," she explains when she sees my shocked expression.

"She's a brute." Keith's smile lights his eyes behind gold-rimmed glasses. "It's great." Keith Zary is vice president of Research for

Jackson & Perkins, the country's largest rose purveyor and cause of many a rose lover's obsession.

I stopped by J&P's research facility in Somos, near Los Angeles, after my visit with Rachel and Phil. I'd been impressed with Rachel's affection for the cream and pink Keith Zary hybrid tea named 'Gemini'. As it turns out, 'Gemini' is Keith's favorite among his own roses. He says that the plant's qualities were apparent so early in the breeding process that it was immediately flagged for reproduction. Evidently, 'Gemini' took the rose exhibition world by storm when it was introduced in 2000. According to Bob Martin, who keeps track of exhibition statistics, 'Gemini' won more Queens of Show from 2000 to 2004 than any other hybrid tea. In 2005 it won the ARS Members' Choice Award.

J&P has bred hundreds of rose-show hybrid tea Queens and won more All-America Rose Selections (AARS) awards — sixty-three and counting — than any other American nursery. The AARS competition, which was begun in 1938 by the ARS, is one of many rose assessments that take place around the world annually. In countries as far flung as South Africa and the Netherlands, new roses are evaluated in test gardens for one to three years. Judges examine everything from bloom color to disease resistance. Top scorers go on to decorate the pages of the world's rose catalogs and color our gardens. Losers are dug up and trashed. Some other flowers, including tulips and carnations, are also tested in international trials, yet only the rose competes in as many contests held in so many countries. We love the Queen of Flowers, but we make her work for our adoration.

With seven AARS awards to his name, Keith is well on his way to matching the AARS record of twenty-four wins set by J&P's famed hybridizer, the late Bill Warriner.

'Gemini' may be Keith's favorite because its blossoms are paler than the other prize-winning roses he has created. White, you see, is his preferred color.

"Whereas I like roses that go 'Bam!'" Debbie has stopped her ruthless culling and come over to chat beside a greenhouse bench covered in two-year-old roses. "Big, bold, loud." She says this with her hands on blue-jeaned hips, honey hair atumble.

"I prefer pastel," insists Keith.

Debbie and Keith regard each other. They grin. He says, "Having different taste in roses works. We miss fewer potential beauties."

Keith began his career breeding peas and beans. Peas and beans offer a certain fascination; after all, Gregor Mendel learned a lot about heredity by studying succeeding generations of peas. But in 1985, when Keith spotted an advertisement in *American Vegetable Grower* magazine for an assistant director of Research for Jackson & Perkins, he applied immediately. He says that it looked like fun, which wasn't an attribute he associated with legumes. Keith, who is a Californian by way of Canada and Minnesota, had always loved roses, but he had never thought that anyone actually bred them and made a living.

"Roses are the most perfect of perennials. They bloom all season. They flower prolifically. They have fragrance. They have amazing colors. They have amazing flower forms. They come in every size from dwarf to climber. They are the most rewarding and the toughest of plants." He shakes his head. "What could be better than this job? I still have a copy of that ad."

Keith's job interview consisted of making rose selections with Bill Warriner. "It seemed so natural to walk through the grow house choosing roses with Bill. I told him that this job was created for me." Warriner must have agreed. Keith was hired as his assistant and became chief hybridizer when Warriner retired in 1988.

JACKSON & PERKINS WAS founded as a wholesale fruit company in 1872 by Charles Perkins, a lawyer who loved to garden, and his father-in-law, A. E. Jackson, who provided financial backing. The company sold strawberries and grapes until one fateful evening when Perkins read *The Rose* by H. B. Ellwanger, who bemoaned America's lack of rosarians.

Almost all the roses that Americans grew throughout the nineteenth century were created by British and European breeders. The popular noisette, offspring of 'Champneys' Pink Cluster', America's first hybridized species, was created and sold back to us by the French. Even the famous 'American Beauty', now celebrated as America's National Floral Emblem, began life in France around 1880 as 'Madame Ferdinand Jamin'. After a rechristening by an American nursery, it became one of America's most popular and most expensive greenhouse-grown roses. In 1898 a single stem cost $3.75, the equivalent of more than $83 in today's currency.

Ellwanger, though, saw a shifting balance of power in the nursery business. "In the production of roses, instead of having exhausted the field, we have only just entered it," he wrote. "The future possibilities open to the raiser of new roses are only dawning upon us."

Perkins took the message to heart. He built one greenhouse, then a second, and in 1896 he hired E. Alvin Miller as hybridizer. In 1901 Miller bred a double-flowered pink climbing variety that he really liked. He named it 'Dorothy Perkins' in honor of

Charles Perkins's granddaughter, J&P marketed it, and absolutely everyone bought it. England's National Rose Society even awarded the rose its coveted Nickerson Cup. At that point, J&P gave up fruit for roses.

In retrospect, Perkins chose just the right moment. While Americans grew roses in their backyards and parks, ornamental gardening had largely been the province of the wealthy into the nineteenth century. But by the late nineteenth century a gradually strengthening American economy created a burgeoning middle class with more money to spend on pleasure. Pleasure included growing perfectly useless beautiful flowers. Horticultural societies organized by nurserymen and amateur plant lovers began to host annual flower shows to feed people's curiosity about new and exotic plants. The shows attracted large crowds and high-quality, diverse exhibits by offering awards for excellence. Inevitably, proponents of individual species began to form their own groups and organize their own competitive shows. The American Rose Society was formed in 1892 by a group of rosarians within the American Society of Florists. Their goal was to oust the carnation as the most popular florist flower. They succeeded quickly.

Specialty gardens became the rage. No longer were roses consigned to the herb garden with other useful medications; no longer did they simply flank the front gate. Roses were given their own space. Middle-class Americans planted Italian-style gardens full of noisette roses draped over pergolas, geometrically shaped beds of miniature roses and paths lined with rose standards. Rambling roses were trained along chains. And in the middle of that increasingly important phenomenon, the well-mown lawn? A formal bed of peacock-hued, stiffly pruned hybrid teas.

The more Americans bought roses, the more American hybridizers worked to supply the demand themselves. In 1930 the
United States became the first country in the world to provide
an intellectual property program for plant inventors. The U.S.
Plant Patent Act meant that one could become rich from creating, patenting, and marketing new plant varieties, rather than
selling established ones. The first plant patented was a climbing rose, 'New Dawn', bred in 1930 by Somerset Rose Nursery
of New Jersey. It's still popular, offering scented silver-pink blossoms all season long. Universities expanded their horticultural
research programs. Nurseries hired horticultural scientists. The
number of new varieties multiplied and gardeners bought them
insatiably. The hunger continues unabated. More money spent
means more money available to create new roses. The ARS recognizes fifty-five classes of roses, including ten thousand varieties
of hybrid tea alone.

THERE ARE TWO WAYS to create an entirely new rose. One
involves waiting until a rose plant suddenly sprouts a different-
looking blossom, or sport. One of the most famous American-
bred sports bloomed in 1830 in the garden of a New York attorney
named Richard Harison. Harison grew two yellow species, *Rosa
spinosissima,* or 'Scotch Rose', and *R. foetida.* One day he noticed
that he had a new variant — a large, vigorous, prickly-stemmed
shrub whose vibrant yellow blossoms bloomed early with a spicy
sweet scent. Was it a bee-borne cross? A natural sport? We'll
never know. Yet we do know that 'Harison's Yellow' was a hit as
soon as it appeared in a local nursery. Americans loved it so much
that they stuck cuttings of the rose into halved potatoes and took
them west by wagon train. You can find 'Harison's Yellow' grow-

ing wild today all along the route of the Oregon Trail. The rose also made it to Texas where they renamed it — the Yellow Rose of Texas.

Miniature roses are particularly prone to sporting. Peter Alonso, a southern California exhibitor, has so far found six sports on a pink and yellow Keith Zary miniature named 'Bee's Knees'. He liked one of them enough to propagate by rooting the stem, thereby creating a new variety, which he named 'Erin Alonso' for his daughter.

Before you rush into the garden, though, be forewarned: Not all rooted sports continue to produce the blossoms that captivate you. You have to grow the plant for a while and make cuttings of it to be certain that it will hold its look. By the way, Jim Delahanty, who grows a huge collection of antique polyanthas at his southern California home, refers to sports as "reproduction without sex, or the rose version of the Immaculate Conception."

You can also make a new rose by imitating a bee. This is called hybridizing and it is what Keith Zary and all the major rose breeders do. Roses are hermaphrodites. They contain both male and female reproductive parts. The center of a rose blossom is the gynoecium, or the female part of the rose. The gynoecium is covered with many pistils, each of which is a chubby ovary topped with a knob-shaped stigma. Around the edge of the gynoecium are lots of stamens, which are the male parts of the rose. Each stamen consists of a lozenge-shaped anther on top of a long, thin filament. As a flower opens, the anthers crack open to reveal yellow pollen (sperm), which either falls onto the stigmas in the gynoecium or is carried off to another rose's stigmas by a hungry bee. The rose blossom itself is sitting on a bowl-shaped container called a hypanthium. If pollination is successful, the hypanthium swells with seeds, becoming a rose hip. In the wild, or in your backyard, most rose hips are eaten by squirrels and birds. After passing through their digestive systems, the rose hips are planted in a nice bit of dung fertilizer from which they sprout and become new roses — or not. Nature is an unreliable mistress.

We interfering humans hybridize roses by removing the anthers and all but one petal from the blooms of one rose. In the plant breeding business, this is called emasculation. Then we swab up the pollen of another type of rose and sweep it over the pistil-filled gynoecium of the first rose. Pregnancy is ensured when a hip forms below the blossom. When the hip colors red or orange, we cut it off and harvest the seed. One way or another, sex happens.

At Jackson & Perkins, rose sex happens in a greenhouse that covers more than an acre. Three huge, fragrant glass rooms are filled with eighty-foot-long, waist-high, wheeled greenhouse benches that resemble massive jelly-roll pans. Some of the benches are thicketed in potted roses; others are filled with trays of peat, perlite, and sand into which rose seeds are planted. I have arrived in April, thereby catching the breeding staff in the midst of two distinct steps of the breeding process: pollinating parent roses for this year's crosses and culling year-old roses from last year's crosses.

From April through June each year, Keith and his staff of ten in Somos collect pollen from three hundred parent roses and make one hundred thousand rose crosses. While he is responsible for making the final decision about which roses to cross, Keith says that "ideas are never the domain of one person." So he consults ahead of time with his staff, other breeders, customers, and a network of rosarians around the country who grow and evaluate new J&P roses.

As soon as he has finalized the program for one year, Keith begins to plan for the next. In all cases, he chooses parents that blend the qualities he is looking for that year. In combination, the parents must have the right blossom shape, leaf color, and plant form; they must be disease-resistant hardy growers; their blossom colors must be attractive when mixed; and they must be strong breeders, able to produce abundant hips filled with many seeds, and able to pass their best characteristics on to their children. Most of all, he says, "I am always looking for parents to help solve the problems we see in today's varieties. Disease resistance and fragrance, which is popular again, are at the very top of the goal list for all breeders."

Every September, staff harvest about four hundred thousand seeds and set them in cold storage for eight weeks to increase the likelihood of germination. In December the seeds are planted, and by April of the next year a portion of the eighty-foot benches should be filled with approximately two hundred thousand inch-high seedlings.

Keith walks over to a bench where the evident germination rate reminds me of a bad haircut — thick in some spots, sparse in others. He gently pats a green patch of infant roses.

"I cross more red roses than any other color because they have a lower germination rate." His right hand points an accusing finger at a bald patch. "But you can see that we still didn't get much this year." He bites his lip as he regards the expanse of seedling-free planting medium. "You only need one," he mutters. Then, looking up, "It's like the Hapsburgs."

Debbie and I gaze at him.

"Inbreeding," he clarifies. "Too few red roses bred with each other repeatedly over the centuries. This is the result." He sweeps an arm toward the bad haircut.

"Prominent chins and a tendency to madness," I say. He rewards me with a laugh.

The first cull, which occurs as soon as the seedlings have two real leaves, removes anything stunted, diseased, or simply peculiar. Roses offer genetic surprises that can mess up the most well-considered cross. Squashy shapes, muddy colors, spiny stems, an undisclosed tendency toward powdery mildew surface far more often than not. Once the roses bloom, Debbie culls them down to two thousand unique varieties. That's what she was doing when Keith and I walked in, "cutting out the dogs," as she calls it. "It can be difficult if you get emotional about them, so I try to stay cold and factual when I do it. I am getting rid of material that isn't good enough."

Ten to twenty plants are propagated by cuttings from each of the two thousand hopefuls and sent to J&P's production fields in Wasco, near Bakersfield. Think of them as a group of classmates, such as the Class of 2003. During the next five years, the Class of 2003 will commute between the greenhouse and fields in Wasco and in Medford, Oregon, near J&P's headquarters. They are propagated and examined repeatedly. By the seventh year, 150 of the 2,000 varieties remain. In the eighth year, Keith and his staff present sixty to seventy-five of those roses to J&P's Marketing Department. This is when the process becomes painful.

Keith and his staff love all the roses they present to Marketing, but no more than ten will be chosen. Not even the country's largest rose wholesaler can afford to mass propagate, advertise, and ship all its deserving roses.

"Once Marketing rejects it, we destroy it."

Part of the difficulty results from culture clash. Marketing types are not necessarily rose lovers. Plant scientists have more faith in flora than in market analyses of popular colors, scents, growth habit, and varieties. And, of course, there is the control issue. It is one thing to cull your own roses for eight years, quite another to cede final selection to people who lack dirt under their fingernails.

Keith's frustration with corporate control peaked in 1998 when he developed a floribunda blessed with sumptuous clusters of creamy apricot-tinged blossoms and a light, spicy scent.

"He won't tell you, so I will." Debbie steps in front of Keith, who crosses his arms and half turns away as she speaks. "He begged them to choose it, just begged them. But no, pale wasn't *in* that year."

Convinced of the rose's quality, Keith submitted one bush to the European rose trials before destroying the rest of the plants at the J&P greenhouses. It won the Golden Rose of The Hague Trophy, which many consider to be the world's highest rose honor. Only one other American-bred rose, 'Queen Elizabeth' bred by Lammerts, has ever won the award. That was in 1954.

"That's when Marketing called, wanted to know if I had any left." Keith radiates residual anger as he picks up the story. "I said, 'No. Remember? You rejected that rose. I destroyed them.'"

"They had hysterics." Debbie wriggles with pleasure. Keith almost smiles.

As it turned out, he had planted two bushes in a neighbor's yard. The genetic stock was saved. J&P introduced the rose, named 'Grand Prize', in 2003. It sells admirably. And now, says Keith, "My boss can't tell a plant from a dog, but he has put new rose people in Marketing who appreciate our work."

It might be simpler to toil alone. Simpler, but chancier.

MANY ROSE GROWERS give hybridizing a try, for as John Mattia says, "It's every rosarian's dream to create his own rose." You can spot the garden of an amateur hybridizer easily. It's the one in which, during peak rose season, the most attractive rose bushes are covered with a mess of labels, cheesecloth, paper bags, and old panty hose. If you are pollinating in the great outdoors, you see, you need to keep a bee from coming along and messing up your careful rose cross. Thus, after impregnating your choicest rose flowers, you cover them until pregnancy is assured.

In 2003 John crossed two hybrid teas, 'Signature' and 'Pretoria', to produce a tall hybrid tea with long, strong stems whose classically shaped four-inch white blossoms are edged in soft cherry. No scent. Remember, John doesn't care about scent. Yet real beauty.

But for the amateur hybridizer, what then? To be picked up by a wholesaler, a rose must be noticed. Yet very few amateurs have won a national or international rose trial, either of which ensures recognition. Even fewer have persuaded a rose wholesaler to pick up, produce, and sell their creation. The problem is the need to guarantee profit.

John was contemplating what to do about his rose when Elizabeth Park's rosarian, Donna Fuss, called to bemoan the cost of commissioning a rose to celebrate the park's centennial, planned for 2004. John gave his rose to the park, which boasts

America's oldest municipal rose garden; the 'Elizabeth Park Centennial' was planted in a place of honor.

Bob Martin, who ships his budwood around in cigar boxes, uses a different approach to get his own successful crosses into production. He sends them to friends. Admittedly, he also has an eye for a marketable rose. Bob bred the pink-blend J&P hybrid tea 'Anne Morrow Lindbergh' with a creamy yellow miniature named 'Fairhope'. In 2002 the result was a mini-flora named 'Butter Cream'. In 2004 he used the same cross and produced a white mini-flora that he named 'Peter Cottontail'. Both his creations are known for their floriferousness. "I want flowers on my roses, lots of flowers. If I wanted foliage, I'd grow holly!"

Bob, who maintains a Pasadena law practice despite living in Arizona, applies for trademark registration on his best creations. He then sends cuttings of the roses to exhibiting friends all over the country. They grow the rose, and if they love it, they show the rose. If the rose is really good, it will win *something,* be it blue ribbon or Queen. Remember, a prize-winning rose has financial potential. Two of Bob's roses, 'Peter Cottontail' and 'Butter Cream' have won enough that they are sold nationally by RoseMania, the same online rose retailer that sells John Mattia's digital rose art.

A lucky story for one amateur hybridizer, but what about the amateurs who want to become independent professionals? The few independents who succeed in the hybridizing business today tend to have excellent connections, some money, a touch of hubris, and an excessive degree of determination. They also specialize. Frank Benardella, former president of the American Rose Society, is one of the country's best-known independent hybridizers. He specializes in miniatures covered in tiny hybrid tea blossoms. He is also a member of Clarence's Secondary Products Company, which provided me with instant access.

Frank is a tall, rangy, barrel-chested man in his early seventies. His ruddy, big-boned face looks imposing when serious and sweet when smiling. Right now, we're in the greenhouse. He is serious.

"See? Nothing." He points to two half-inch seedlings in the upper right corner of a planting tray. They are lonely green sentinels on a plain of brown potting soil. "I took the tray out of the refrigerator six days ago. Normally they shoot up like hair on a dog."

Unlike Keith Zary, Frank plants and waters his seed before giving it six weeks of cold treatment in a refrigerator where the temperature is — or should be — about 32 degrees F.

"I think they froze," he says. This would be the second time that Frank's seeds have frozen. He bought a high-tech thermostat for the rose refrigerator after his seeds iced four years ago. So much for technology.

Frank came to roses by way of Goody hair-care products.

"Goody, as in the clip that is holding my hair right now?"

"Probably."

"What did you do for Goody?"

"I headed up product development."

"So you know a lot about what women do to their hair."

"Yes." He hedges. "At least when it comes to hairbrushes and barrettes."

He knew enough that when he retired in 1994, Frank was senior vice president of International Sales and Marketing.

Frank's passion for roses began in 1957 when he bought some for his mother-in-law and succumbed to them himself. The following year he was captured by a Jackson & Perkins installment-purchase plan. If he could convince others to order roses, he would be paid in plants. Frank is a persuasive man who pats shoulders readily. Soon he had a rose garden, and he and his wife, June, had helped form the Garden State Rose Society, which was as social as it was educational.

"A lot of us had young children," says June. "The children played together. We visited on the weekends. You know, 'You see my rose garden, I'll see your rose garden, then we'll have a barbecue.'"

Frank's first exhibiting win was also key.

"After you win at the local level, you want to win at the district level. After that you say, 'This is fun,' and you have to go to the nationals." Frank is beaming.

"Frank has a very competitive nature," says June. Frank looks surprised.

The Benardellas have two daughters and, at the time they grew six hundred — or was it eight hundred? — roses. He traveled a lot for work, but he explains, "I planned my trips overseas when there were lulls in the growing season. I always went to the Orient in November when the roses calmed down and to Europe in February when they were dormant."

In between Frank's business trips, the entire family traveled for roses.

"The national rose conventions were our vacations," explains June. They tried to make the trips educational. After an Atlanta conference, they toured the Coca-Cola factory; in Detroit, they visited Ford Motors.

"In Milwaukee we went to a brewery," remembers Frank.

June has enjoyed the travel — well, perhaps not the twenty-seven-hour nonstop drive they once made to Colorado with two young daughters and eighty show blooms. But more recent trips to the rose trials in Japan, Holland, and South Africa — Frank judges flowers while she wanders around the beds breathing in the scented air — have been wonderful. Mostly, though, she loves the people. "Rose people are just . . . well, they are just the kindest, most generous, most interesting people. Oh gosh, except I'm not saying that about Frank and myself! It's other rose people who are that way."

More benefits? "Frank brings flowers in from the greenhouse in the winter." Then haltingly, "Of course, it all rather does away with ever taking an ordinary vacation. We *have* talked about it. 'Seashore this year or rose convention? Mountains or rose convention?' The rose convention always wins."

Suddenly she says, "Do you know what I did yesterday? I went to a dog show. Frank wouldn't be caught dead at a dog show." Pause. "It was fun."

By the late 1970s Frank had won almost all of the most prestigious awards at the ARS Spring and Fall Nationals and served a term as ARS president. His fingers uncurl from his right fist as he counts the accomplishments. "What was left?" he asks rhetorically. Both hands splay open. He could easily palm a basketball. "I said, 'Let's do hybridizing!' "

Frank is a self-described hybrid tea nut. So in 1980, his first year as a brand-new hybridizer, he built a fourteen-by-thirty-six-foot lean-to onto the side of the house and tried his hand at breeding his favorite type of rose.

"How did it go?"

He hesitates before answering. "I learned a lot," he says finally. "The next year I switched to minis."

Frank Benardella may be a hybrid tea nut, but he is realistic.

And agreeing with June, he says, "I guess I am competitive." The market dominance of hybrid teas and floribundas means that many companies have established track records. How could incipient breeder Frank Benardella claim his own territory? His thoughts turned to the miniatures that he and June grew in their mixed perennial garden.

"They're hardy, ever-blooming, colorful," explains Frank. "They're versatile. They're relatively carefree. I realized that I liked everything about them except the shape of the flower."

A word about miniatures. They are natural dwarfs that grow one to two feet high, although there are also micro-minis that are just three inches high and a few climbers with tiny leaves and blossoms that grow to ten feet. The Western world discovered miniatures after the English took the island of Mauritius from the French in 1810. Soon the rose that British botanists found growing all over the island was the newest fashion in English gardens. By 1840 it had arrived in America.

Until Frank Benardella turned his attention to them, the most famous hybridizers of miniature roses in America were the eminent Ralph Moore and the late Dee Bennett, a woman in the male-dominated world of rose hybridizing. They both propelled the popularity of miniature roses by creating healthy, attractive shrubs in a range of colors never before seen. Moore, in particular, is fascinated by old roses and has introduced the look of crested-blossom moss roses and clustered-blossom floribundas into his miniatures. Frank Benardella chose to transform the miniature rose blossom into a high-center, symmetrical bloom, in other words, a tiny hybrid tea.

The seriousness of Frank's 1980 decision to become a breeder is signaled by the fact that he built a greenhouse immediately. No panty hose and paper bags for him. Frank built his current, state-of-the-art greenhouse after his retirement, when he and June moved into an idyllic fieldstone and white-frame oversized cottage set on twenty-five pond-splashed acres in central New Jersey. The greenhouse is a fifty-by-fifty-foot peak-roofed, translucent polycarbonate structure attached to a large, green metal utility building. It's just visible behind a copse of evergreens about fifty feet from the house.

Inside, on eight twenty-foot-long rolling metal tables, unfurling seedlings carpet black plastic trays, baby roses green two-and-a-half-inch and five-and-a-half-inch plastic pots. Each of the larger pots also sports a quarter-inch-diameter green dowel bedecked with a rainbow of tiny translucent plastic clothespins. This is Frank's point system. Frank awards clothespins when he spots something he really likes, such as a perfectly shaped blossom or an interesting color. The more clothespins, the better the plant and the greater its chance of surviving until the final trial, which is to spend a year in Frank's test garden behind the greenhouse. Against the far wall is a bank of hybrid teas and shrub-sized miniatures planted in white twenty-gallon buckets that once contained joint compound.

Frank wipes pollen from small-flowered hybrid teas onto miniature roses (usually Benardella minis) when he breeds miniatures, because he believes that miniature mother plants produce more miniatures than hybrid tea mother plants. When he makes his parent choices, he emphasizes hybrid teas with good flower form and miniatures with good plant shape and above-average hip production. At the 2003 ARS Fall National, he won the Rose Hybridizers' Association Trophy for a seedling cross between

'Kristin' and a German-bred hybrid tea named 'Laguna', which is one of his favorite studs.

We walk over to the bank of hybrid teas in joint compound buckets, which, it turns out, is the Benardella stud farm. He cups his hand around a 'Laguna' blossom, whose deep yellow petals are brushed with red.

"Nice, don't you think?"

The "Nice, don't you think?" resonates with affection and, after so many successful crosses, with gratitude. 'Laguna' reliably passes on its attractive, upright shape and a genetic heritage of bright, clear petal color. Some of its children have red blossoms, some yellow, some bicolor — all of them are vibrant.

Bob Martin describes Frank's roses as "Mini-Queen machines." Both 'Kristin' and 'Soroptimist International' appear in the top ten on his Web site tally of ARS Miniature Queens from 2000 to 2004. Lots of exhibitors at the upcoming ARS Spring National will be trying to win with Benardella minis.

Yet Frank shakes his head when congratulated. "I'm not saying that my roses are right. In fact, oftentimes I think they are wrong. When you breed for perfect form and so forth, you are losing other traits, like lots of fragrance or lots of bloom."

Frank won't quite agree with John Mattia, who says, "Let's be honest, hybridizing is a crapshoot." But with a Mona Lisa smile, he offers, "The parentage listed for hybrid roses isn't always true." Rose breeders spend a lot of time researching the genetic heritage of the roses from which they breed, searching for the dominant traits that will be passed on. If breeders listed every single cross they used to create a rose, their creation could be more easily copied.

Frank breeds roses for two different markets. The first is the Japanese, European, and South African miniature cut-flower market. I tell him that I've never heard of miniature cut flowers.

"They're a huge business overseas where they're used a lot in bouquets. For that market, I'm looking for small perfect blooms on nine-inch stems. I also breed them to have long-lasting blooms. They should last at least a week in a vase."

For the American market, he strives for a vigorous, well-rounded plant that produces lots of perfectly formed blooms and grows well in the garden. He sells them primarily through the specialist nursery, Nor'East Miniature Roses, although other specialists, such as Bridges Roses, and national nurseries including Jackson & Perkins stock his roses. Knowing that prize winners sell best, he often enters the ARS Award of Excellence trials, which he has won ten times so far.

At this point Frank reaches over and stirs the tray of presumably frozen seed with a long forefinger. I realize that he has been staring at it while telling me about his winning miniatures.

"You wish your life away when you're hybridizing," he says. "First, you're planning in your mind the crosses you want to make for the year. You do those crosses. Gather the seeds. You've got to wait until the next year for those seeds to germinate. You can't wait for the first bloom. Then you throw most of them away. You never get the look you are trying to achieve. Not quite. But you are always searching."

5

"I've Always Been, Shall We Say, Competitive"

"This bud here, see? You take that off." Dr. Tommy Cairns's right thumb and forefinger press briefly together. A nascent rosebud drops to the ground. "And here." He removes another bud forming between stem and leaf. "And here and here again." Pea-sized buds rain onto the redwood-chip path.

Tommy's fingers abruptly cease squeezing. Only one bud — the future show bloom — remains at the tip of the stem. He straightens. "This is 'Kristin'. But you recognize her, don't you?"

"Yes." I'm startled into a lie. Tommy is as exacting as he is charming and I don't want to dissatisfy him. To salve my conscience, I offer what I do know. "Frank Benardella's rose." Tommy nods. His hands caress the small vaselike form.

"Amazing that he gets this. Such style. And look at the foliage." He bends an Irish-green leaf toward me.

I take a deep breath and admit, "It's hard for me to recognize some of these roses when they aren't in bloom." How about *any* of the roses?

"Of course." Tommy's square pale face gentles in sympathy. "But you will learn." A directive rather than reassurance.

The day after I met Keith Zary at Jackson & Perkins, Tommy invited me into the garden that he shares with his companion, Luis Desamero. Tommy is the current president of the World Federation of Rose Societies and a former president of the American Rose Society. He's also a semiretired forensic chemist who spent twenty-two years at the U.S. Food and Drug Administration, where he was director of the National Center for Toxicology Research. Luis was an accountant for Lytton Industries before his retirement. In the rose world, he is best known as a talented rosarian, gourmet chef, and classical pianist.

The Spring National in San Diego is just five weeks away. At this point, exhibitors are deep into preshow rose care. Tommy Cairns is disbudding roses.

Tommy and Luis grow over one thousand rose plants with which they have won a roomful of awards. Literally. It's the first room you enter at the back of the house after leaving the garden. Tommy calls it the Ego Room. The walls are invisible behind plaques and pictures and framed certificates. A linear froth of blue, red, white, and yellow ribbons — mostly blue — covers the join where walls and ceiling meet. Tables are decorated with crystal jars and vases. It's their haul from over thirty years of exhibiting roses.

Tommy and Luis exhibit all kinds of roses, including antiques, but they are best known for their hybrid teas, floribundas, and miniatures. They hold the current record for national miniature-rose trophies awarded in the United States. They also routinely fly with their roses to England and win Britain's All-Miniature Show. The plethora of awards, and the talent that they signify, have made Tommy and Luis famous in the rose world. They both have roses named for them: 'Luis Desamero' is an eighteen-inch miniature with fruit-scented, pale yellow blossoms; 'Editor Tommy Cairns' is a faintly scented pink and white blend hybrid tea.

If one thousand roses summon the image of an expansive rainbow landscape bordered in emerald lawn, you'd be wrong. Tommy and Luis own a stucco house on a steep patch of hillside on one of Laurel Canyon Boulevard's corkscrew turns. Now that I think about it, their home is the California equivalent of Clarence's home in Maine. Both are smallish, attractively ordinary houses hidden for much of the summer behind an explosion of container-raised flowers. The car-stopping nature of the display means that each is a threat to public safety. Clarence, at least, is on a straight section of street. Tommy and Luis have the opportunity to cause mayhem on a blind curve.

"What do you think?" Tommy's right foot, shod in brown loafer, taps as he awaits my answer. Standing still on a sunny Saturday, evidently relaxed in blue jeans and white T-shirt, Tommy seems to vibrate. "I am an A-1 type of person," he explains. Actually, he says *pairson*. Tommy is from Scotland.

"Goodness." I'm overwhelmed by the number of roses. Their yard looks like a cross between a production nursery and a one-species demonstration garden.

Behind Tommy, Luis chuckles softly. "It is a lot, isn't it?"

Luis is a small, slender man with intense dark eyes, a thatch of black hair, and an aura of calm. On this day, the hair is covered in a wide-brimmed hat. He wears long khaki shorts and a red cotton plaid shirt that is untucked. His hands are armored in heavy thorn-proof gloves. He has been dragging twenty-gallon container plants around while Tommy taught me how to disbud roses.

Tommy and Luis pruned their roses in December and January, earlier than Rachel, because their climate is warmer. At this point the plants should be covered in big green buds and decorated with healthy, disease- and insect-free foliage. They look perfect to me.

When Tommy bought the house thirty-five years ago, he liked everything about it except the garden.

"I was inundated with snails," he says, conjuring scenes from a sci-fi horror film. "I had to find something that the little buggers wouldn't devour." He thought of roses because the British always think of roses. Tommy planted a dozen hybrid teas in the back yard. The snails slimed away. Within a year, twelve plants had bloomed into a hundred.

"I call it the vanishing lawn syndrome. I planted roses, and with every one I planted I needed more and more."

Tommy's obsession might have stayed in the garden had he not brought a bucket of blossoms into the office. Tommy, who admits that he is not modest, gloated about his flowers as he showed them around. A colleague remarked that they might be pretty, but they would never win trophies at an upcoming show.

"Well, you know, I have always been, shall we say, competitive. Tennis, soccer — I have always wanted to win. So I took that bucket of roses to the show and came home with four trophies."

COMPETITIVENESS IS THE dominant personality trait of most rose exhibitors. I am so noncompetitive that I don't even like to keep score during card games that I win. This may be why I was surprisingly slow to recognize its importance. Rachel Hunter had described her drive to be the best typist – race car driver – rose exhibitor. John Mattia had told me that he subjects himself to the pain of losing "because you might win." Yet exhibitors are extraordinarily friendly and flower happy; their welcoming, cheerful plant talk lulled me into thinking that they show roses simply because it's fun. That's what they said when I asked: *because it's fun.* I didn't get it until I heard the steel in Tommy Cairns's voice when he said, "So I took that bucket of roses to the show and came home with four trophies." Tommy loves everything about roses, and he and Luis would grow them no matter what. But *damn,* he does love to grow *the* best rose and bring home a Queen. Better yet, bring home all the trophies.

I began to ask exhibitors, "Are you competitive in general?"

"Yes, of course." This was often said with eyebrows raised as if *isn't everyone?*

Bob Martin said, "I just like to be the best."

At his very first rose show, he cut a "particularly excellent" specimen of a red blend hybrid tea named 'Double Delight', bypassed the novice category, and entered it in the hybrid tea class from which Queen is chosen. The rose won a blue ribbon.

"Well, it was Tommy Cairns who won Queen and Best in Show and almost everything else that day," remembers Bob. "He came up and asked me why I had entered my rose in a major category instead of the novice class. I didn't know him from Adam at the time, but I looked him in the eye and said, 'That's because, from what I can tell, you're the best and I want to beat you.'"

The urge to defeat another and the desire to achieve are synergistic motives that keep us coming back, whether to the race course, card table, dart board, or rose garden. Beating a competitor provides an immediate visceral thrill; winning offers lasting pride. Many rosarians believe that competition drives them toward perfection, or at least toward improvement, and helps them focus on what they need to do better in the garden. Knowing that the Day of Judgment will arrive, when their ability, perseverance, and enthusiasm will be evaluated, they strive to choose the best roses and grow them more skillfully than before. A major win acknowledges that yes, they did do the best possible job.

But does it? Any triumph that relies on judges is potentially biased; think of how often the scoring of Olympic ice skating and diving events incites controversy. Geri Minot McCarron avoided the Nationals throughout the 1990s because she felt it was "incongruous" to be judged in an important event that "depends somewhat on the subjective opinions of judges." She will attend this year's Spring National because she's made that pact with Rachel Hunter, but she frets about the validity of a sport that involves flowers grown in a wide variety of gardens, uncontrollable weather, and human judges instead of clocks. Geri was on her college swim team, and in addition to teaching English, she has transformed high school track-and-field athletes into winners. "In those events, the stopwatch, tape measure, and AccuTrack photos are precise." She believes that everyone in such events has "a level playing field."

That's not true for rose competition. Soil preparation, plant selection, garden care, weather, and the design of the bloom transportation box are just a few of the variables with which competitors contend before they even encounter the judges. However, in Geri's track-and-field events, one athlete in the fifty-yard dash may have eaten an inadequate breakfast and another might have a cold. While a stopwatch regularizes the scoring, the playing field is never truly level in any sport.

Geri says that she has finally come to understand this, although she may never fully accept it. Curiously, her change of heart happened in a calculus course that she took a few years ago.

"I taught high school English by day, took the math class at night, and spent endless weekends in the library." Rose care happened at 11 p.m. In the midst of differential equations, she recalls, "I understood how small variables can produce big changes, and I learned not to expect that I could ever control all the variables that affect my garden." She may still bemoan the lack of Accu-Track photos in rose competition, but on May 8 Geri will take her place at the starting gate.

Winning a marathon or rose show Queen is a manifestation of the pursuit of excellence. As Charles Murray writes so eloquently in his book *Human Accomplishment,* while we each honor equality, we also long to reach beyond the norm and achieve something — be it inventing the wheel, hand-knitting argyle socks, or growing and grooming an exquisite hybrid tea. We identify a skill, take courage by the hand, and try our best.

Although a perfect flower does not seem as significant as the wheel, it may serve a particular need. In 2005 Rutgers University geneticist Terry McGuire demonstrated that we are more likely to smile when we receive flowers than when given something else. Ancient artifacts reveal that humans have wanted to fashion loveliness almost as long as they have wanted to savor it. As Murray writes, we evince "an impulse to create something that has no purpose but to be pleasing to the human eye or ear, to our sense of taste or touch, to our internal sense of what is beautiful. A lucky few of us are able to create beauty; all of us have some corner in our souls that yearns for it."

FOR TOMMY AND LUIS, nothing is more beautiful than the rose. As does John Mattia, Tommy often refers to it as the Queen of Flowers. They don't have enough land to grow a thousand roses in the ground. Instead, they raise most of their plants in seven- and fifteen-gallon black plastic pots set tight against each other on redwood benches. It is a regimented profusion of plants. Over the years the driveway has shrunk considerably as they built retaining walls and concrete terraces to hold the floral multitude. Still cramped, they annexed a patch of wasteland above the property whose primary feature is a towering steel pylon that carries high-tension wires. They leveled, terraced, and carpeted the area in redwood bark, which Tommy lauds as an excellent weed suppressant. Then they filled it with roses. Some are in the ground; most are in containers set on two-foot-high redwood benches. The benches actually surround the soaring tower.

"Oh that." Tommy looks up from disbudding one of his ten 'Glowing Amber' miniatures. "I hardly notice it anymore."

Disbudding removes all of the side buds except for the show bloom at the end of each cane. If they concentrate, Tommy or Luis can disbud fifty plants an hour. With a thousand plants, that's twenty hours of steady disbudding. They spread the twenty hours over a week, working in orderly fashion from one end of the garden to the other end. Rosebuds must be removed when they are tiny because removing anything larger than a pea leaves a scar on the stem. A scar is a flaw. Flaws reduce a rose's winning potential. So after the gardenwide disbudding, Tommy and Luis — and Rachel and Phil and all other winning exhibitors — disbud individual rose plants every time they walk through the garden.

Some exhibitors don't disbud floribundas, whose blooms grow in sprays. But Tommy and Luis check their floribunda sprays and may often remove one or more buds to give the remaining buds more room to expand. Again, it must be done early or the darkened end of a stem will remain among the blooms — a sure sign of a beginner or, worse, a lazy exhibitor.

Tommy and Luis are the antithesis of lazy. Luis handles the horticulture; Tommy handles the chemicals. At shows, Luis grooms the miniatures and Tommy grooms the big roses. They are fanatical about rose care, although Tommy prefers the term *disciplined*.

"Roses are easy to grow, but you have to have a disciplined mind. Feeding, pruning, disbudding, deadheading, spraying — you must do your chores when they need doing. When you see the onset of powdery mildew, you must spray immediately, not say, 'Well, I'll do it on Saturday.' By Saturday, it will have taken over the garden. You can't afford a lackadaisical attitude. You have to be disciplined and you need commitment."

This doesn't sound like fun, I say. Tommy disagrees. His accent broadens and gentles as he explains.

"Deadheading, feeding, spraying — they're not really chores; they're how you spend time with the roses. Roses help you shed the stress of the day. They are always beautiful, always interesting, often challenging. But that is fine because I would rather walk into a rose garden and deadhead than take blood-pressure medication."

As Tommy speaks, I realize how often I bemoan gardening's quotidian tasks. On a muddy spring foray, I might spread compost over all five perennial beds, divide striped hostas, inadvertently dig up late tulips, and emerge bloodied from pruning the 'Henry Kelsey' climber. Then, exhausted and somewhat aggrieved about all the effort, I do nothing for days at a time but admire the azalea's pink crepe flowers and watch the burdock grow until it resists removal.

Instead of viewing garden chores as a partnership with my plants, I too often labor like a resentful employee. I weed and deadhead heedlessly, seeing the plant in hand without looking at the garden. And the fantasy day for which I work — full of sunshine and enough free time to relax and admire my handiwork? That day rarely comes. As a consequence, when the first snow whitens the beds, I inevitably wish aloud that I'd had more time to enjoy the garden that summer. But if the chores become part of the pleasure, I might notice summer before it passes. I might appreciate what I do in the garden and value what the garden does for me.

Just as I resolve to improve my attitude, Tommy says, "If you ask the average married woman whose kids are gone to tell you the one thing she wants most, she'll say that she wants a beautiful garden. And a garden cannot be a garden without roses." Case made, he smiles and reaches for a potted mini.

My epiphany dissolves in the flood of Tommy's typically male certainty that he knows what the opposite sex wants. He loves roses and women love flowers; ergo, women must want gardens. Women want time *to* garden, or read or travel or sleep, for pity's sake. Even as I stew, though, I remember the jostling crowd in my local garden center the week before. While men examined lawn tractors and soaker hoses, women trundled flats of pansies toward the checkout counter. Complete strangers shared their planting plans and smiled with springtime enthusiasm. He's right. We do want beautiful gardens, and many of us want roses — easy landscape roses.

"So, do you think about roses all the time?"

"Well . . ." He draws out the word. "It's almost a subliminal thing. A mania for roses transcends all strata of living. I mean, Luis and I even buy toilet paper with roses on it." He offers a brief, half-swallowed laugh. "If we're scanning the television channels and spot a program that's got the word *rose* in the title, it gets our attention. We watch it, whether it's good or not. We can't help it. Some of us are born to be rose people. It's in the genes." Long pause as he judiciously pinches a mini. "I know I shouldn't feel this way, but I wouldn't want everyone to have the rose gene."

He softens the remark by adding that he is honored to be a custodian of roses, but I understand the original sentiment. Private clubs, secret handshakes, and certain accents never go out of fashion. The marines famously offer young men and women a chance to join "the few." We all want to be among the chosen. My grade school class numbered eighteen students; we often were told by our teachers that we were a unique group, able to excel as other classes did not. In retrospect, I realize that each class probably was told the same, but the message worked for me. I felt special, and harder to admit, I felt superior. Did that feel good? Absolutely.

Of course, if few people inherit the rose gene, even fewer become competitive exhibitors. A limited number of potential rivals might be cause for celebration. But many exhibitors bemoan small shows. They are warriors who want the thrill of major battle. Nonetheless, the warrior class seems to be shrinking. Twenty-first-century time demands have decimated the number of people willing to coddle finicky exhibition varieties. Roses are more popular than ever in America, but rose shows are disappearing.

Tommy says that the shows may be fewer and smaller, but they are better. "The standard has been raised, and the average

Joe is unable to meet that standard." He sets down yet one more six-inch pot and stretches. "You'll see what I mean at the Spring National. Five more weeks." His tightly strung body gives an almost imperceptible shiver. "We rose people are indeed wonderful people — outside of the hours of competition."

6

To Spray or Not to Spray

 "When I started, Tommy Cairns told me that I needed to spray every week. *Every week!*" Kitty Belendez's corkscrew of black curls bobs as she shakes her head. "But I agree with him about commitment. When it comes to roses, I'm obsessive."

"Try obsessive about everything." Kitty's husband, Bob, squats down to adjust a metal plant label. He is compact, gray haired and deeply tanned, clad in gray corduroy shorts and gray knit shirt. He is also barefoot — his preferred ambulatory mode. The corners of his eyes behind horn-rimmed dark glasses crinkle. Kitty laughs.

"Well, true."

Kitty is the same height as Bob. She is as round as he is lean and as lively as he is calm. Today, she is dressed in a lilac shirt and white capri pants.

Kitty hands me a copy of the Exhibitor's Rose Care Calendar, which she developed in 2003 as a way to document and regulate how she treated her roses. The single-page calendar, specific to the southern California climate, lists rose-care tasks by the month. According to the chart, next week they will feed their roses with fish emulsion, iron chelate, zinc, Epsom salts, and SuperThrive,

which Kitty describes as "one of those mystical magical elixirs."
They will also disbud daily. Tomorrow they will spray for dis-
ease and insects. All this, because the calendar lists April as Peak
Show Season! The exclamation point is Kitty's.

Kitty and Bob Belendez live about an hour north of Tommy
Cairns in hot, supremely sunny Santa Clarita. Their wood and
brick ranch house on a quiet, tree-lined street is unmistakably
a rosarian's home. Miniatures in pots flank the front door and
garage; hybrid teas crowd the front yard; floribundas populate
the sidewalk strip where everyone else has grass. More hybrid
teas line their driveway, as well as that of their neighbor's parallel
driveway. We walk next door.

"When our former neighbor sold this house, the contract
said, 'You can't touch Kitty's roses. They're prize winners.' The
buyer didn't know anything about roses, but now she's in love
with them. She just adores 'Rina Hugo'." Kitty points to a five-
foot-high shrub covered with fat buds that will open soon into
a carmine pink. "She likes to take bouquets to her kid's teacher.
I tell her she can pick whatever she wants except during show
season." Kitty examines a leaf as she talks, straightens a rose label, separates two close-growing canes and peers in. "Oh, look at
these side buds." She pinches them off with manicured, unpol-
ished fingernails.

Kitty has 310 plants at the moment, including 130 miniatures,
eighty-five hybrid teas, fifty-five floribundas, twenty-five shrubs
and fifteen OGRs. Unlike other rosarians, she is not obsessed
with the shape of the hybrid tea. Instead, she wants colorful,
scented blossoms. Yes, in contrast to John Mattia, Kitty believes
that a rose should perfume the air. The fragrance of a rose contains more than thirty identifiable scents. No wonder they lured

us into submission several millennia ago. Aroma is so important to Kitty that she has underwritten a new Most Fragrant Rose competition at the upcoming Spring National.

I try to compare her roses to Tommy and Luis's but am stymied by the visual difference between the yards — production nursery versus garden with a patch of grass. The foliage on Kitty's roses looks as healthy as the foliage on Tommy's roses. Yet her foliage looks real to me, while Tommy's looked almost artificial in its perfection. Her floribundas are bigger plants with longer canes than Tommy and Luis's. I have no idea what difference this will make on May 8.

As we lean over, head to head, to examine a cane, Kitty says, "For the past couple of years, we've been getting foliage damage that baffled me. I was sure it was something that I sprayed." She worried that she would have to stop each chemical in turn and examine the results; withholding an essential chemical might welcome pests or disease, which could ruin her chances at the Spring National. Just in time, she figured out that the culprit was Preen, a preemergent herbicide that kills weeds before they sprout. She had been using a lot of it.

"She was like the Preen Fairy, throwing the stuff around like it was gold dust," comments Bob.

"I had my mask on and everything, but I was out there sprinkling it over everything — la-di-dah-di-dah." Kitty demonstrates with a twirl, her arms flinging imaginary herbicide. When the foliage shriveled, Kitty powered up her computer and learned that Preen should be spread on the soil, not on leaves. "After all, you don't have weeds on your foliage." Kitty shakes her head. "So I do screw up, but I try to learn and correct my mistakes."

In the backyard, Kitty and Bob have a kidney-shaped pool,

another diminutive patch of grass, a peach tree — "and that weed," says Bob.

"What weed?" Kitty whirls toward him, clearly horrified after our discussion of Preen. Bob points to a dianthus planted beneath the peach tree. She relaxes. "Oh, that. Our daughter, Tina, gives me birthday plants. We keep them until we kill them."

While exhibitors' gardens like Kitty's are not sullied by other flora, roses grow well with companions such as dianthus. In fact, taking roses out of a monoculture often reduces the pests and disease that trouble traditional plantings. Stephen Scanniello, former director of the Brooklyn Botanic Garden's Cranford Rose Garden, recommends that northern gardeners surround their roses with short evergreens such as boxwood for winter color. Spring bulbs such as narcissus and grape hyacinth complement newly emerging foliage; gray and blue shades of lavender, salvia, rosemary, and nepeta (catmint) highlight pink blossoms; and asters and chrysanthemums "can be used to hide the inevitable naked knees of hybrid teas in autumn as they go into their cool-weather cycle of bloom." Whatever companions you select, though, don't crowd everything together; all roses require good air circulation.

Tina may be trying to subvert her parents' yard with dianthus because they have lured her daughter Nani into rose fascination. It's not that Tina dislikes roses. She's fond enough of them to care for the garden when her parents are away at shows, although the degree of her mother's obsession does cause Tina to roll her eyes. No, it's just that Kitty and Bob have been taking their granddaughter to rose shows since she was in a stroller. At age twenty-two, Nani's schedule keeps her from attending as many shows as she used to, but she makes a point to accompany her grandparents to the local Santa Clarita show each year.

"It's a long walk from the prep area to the exhibit hall, so she helps carry in our roses." Kitty pulls dead stems off the dianthus as she speaks. "She'll critique the specimens — 'Grandma, why are you putting this in?' and 'Look at this foliage. It's all messed up!' I call her Miss Smartypants." Kitty straightens. She's smiling. "I guess we've made an impression."

Needless to say, Kitty and Bob's backyard is as inundated with scented bloom as the front yard. Miniatures spill from black and clay-colored plastic pots. David Austin and old-garden climbers color a white trellis fence. Antique roses are planted along the concrete pathway on the right side of the house. We dodge 'Anna de Diesbach', a strongly scented, pink hybrid perpetual climber from 1858.

"We chopped her down hard this year and now look." The rose is clambering up its arch. Kitty and Bob won the Dorothy C. Stemler Memorial at the 2002 Spring National with 'Anna de Diesbach'. They also won the Dowager Queen that year with another old French rose, 'Yolande d'Aragon'.

The path to the left of the house is known as Death Row. It's where the roses go when they're on their way out. Kitty doesn't include the plants on Death Row in her rose count. Nor does she include grafted seedlings or her hybridizing experiments. In 1992 she crossed 'Winter Magic' with 'Hurdy Gurdy' and produced a pretty little white miniature with a pink picotee edging. She has never bothered to register the rose, but she has won Best Seedling awards with it at local shows. At the moment, 120-inch-tall seedlings — the result of last year's crosses — rest in the shade of a gazebo outside the back door of the house.

"There's another two hundred of these in the garage," groans Bob, adding that the garage is so crowded with rose stuff that he parks his blue van in the driveway. Kitty doesn't include any of the cuttings or rose-cross seedlings in her count.

"That's because she doesn't know how to count," Bob mutters.

"He's just grumpy because he knows that if I grow them, I keep them for five years." Kitty turns to me and explains in a rosarian-being-reasonable voice. "I need five years to be able to evaluate them properly."

"And then we keep them anyway. You always lie about how many roses we actually take care of."

"Well . . ." Kitty drags out the word as she considers. "True." She smiles and shrugs.

Kitty bought her first roses in 1985, just two of them and she's not sure why. She had tried collecting geraniums but found them boring. She tried camellias and azaleas, but they don't bloom year-round, so her interest "fizzled." But the roses flowered continuously, so when she received a notice for the 1986 ARS Pacific Southwest District Rose Convention in Pasadena, she told Bob, "Let's go see what this is all about."

"Well, we went to the convention and I walked into the show-room and said, 'Oh my God.' I had never seen so many roses in my life." Kitty saw bouquets of a red-blend hybrid tea named 'Double Delight', leaned in to sniff its spicy fragrance, and said "I've got to have that; I have *got* to have that."

So that was that. They dug up the yard. Or rather, Bob dug up the yard.

"Everything is roses now," says Kitty — rose shows, rose society presidency, rose photography, rose Web pages, award-winning rose-related writing. She has roses outside the house. And, as do most exhibitors, she has roses inside the house, although she never cuts a bouquet to take indoors. "If you have roses that are beautiful enough to display, they're going to a show." Instead, rose-patterned wallpaper covers their kitchen walls; a rose-patterned clock ticks quietly above the breakfast table; a basket of pink silk roses decorates the top of the refrigerator. Tommy Cairns is right. A mania for roses does transcend all strata of living.

Of necessity, much of Bob's life is also roses. Bob is a retired long-haul truck driver who sometimes still yearns for the open road. His ongoing commentary about their life in roses is long-suffering and deeply affectionate, and it makes Kitty laugh. Besides living with a woman gone mad for roses, Bob prunes and deadheads and digs holes for new plants. He drives to competitions at ridiculous hours and helps do whatever Kitty asks him to do — fill vases, polish leaves, complete labels, bring her coffee. Once he stopped in Grand Saline, Texas, midhaul between California and Louisiana to pick up three Joe Winchel hybrid teas named 'Dorothy Anne' in honor of Winchel's wife. Dorothy Anne herself drove up the long road from nursery to highway to hand them to Bob. He put them in his sleeping compartment, continued his route to Shreveport, and then drove home to Santa Clarita. "I kept thinking, 'If I kill these, she's going to kill me.'"

Bob also prepares Kitty's sprayer, although he can't abide chemicals. In truth, Kitty can't abide them either. When she first began to show roses, Kitty followed the advice she received to spray weekly, only to find that her roses suffered. The more she sprayed, the more diseases appeared. She switched chemicals frequently to keep her roses from developing resistance; still, the plants struggled. Frustrated, she researched chemical-free approaches. She now uses an organic horticultural oil to protect her plants during dormancy but says, "I don't want to be an organic gardener."

"I've seen the gardens of people who claim to be organic and they're not going to win Queen of Show, not even going to win a lot of trophies." She shakes her head. I nod, although inwardly I cringe at the aptness of her comment.

Even though the fish fertilizer and compost tea with which I feed my roses keeps them healthy, they still suffer an occasional bout of blackspot in Maine's foggy summers. I usually pick off the diseased leaves instead of using a chemical, which means that the long canes of the ramblers can look defoliated. Kitty is right; such roses will never win awards.

Claude Graves, who had described intransigent old-rose and modern-rose advocates as rose snobs, says that organic gardeners have a high tolerance for pain.

"How bad are you willing to have your roses look?" Before I can answer, he continues, "Frankly, I'd go crazy if my roses were in the kind of shape that the pure organic people allow."

Generally I don't mind what Claude portrays as "a pretty good scattering of yellow leaves," but now that I've spent time among serious rosarians, I'm torn. I still am committed to saving the earth with organics, but I'm jealous of Kitty's gorgeous plants. They're thick with shiny foliage and fat buds.

Kitty sprays a fungicide and insecticide every other week from March until show season. She stops during the summer, when she repels spider mites with a water-only spray. She starts the chemicals again in mid-September to prepare the roses for the fall shows.

"Bottom line is that I spray no more than twelve times a year." Kitty is adamant that exhibitors do not poison the planet by over-using chemicals. The advent of new varieties of disease- and pest-resistant roses certainly has enabled them to spray much less than they once did. Yet the phrase "thermonuclear spray program" does crop up on exhibitors' Web forums. The exhibitors' guide to chemicals on Bob Martin's Web site is six pages long. And during an ARS Yankee District meeting a couple of years ago, "Making the Most of Fungicides" had a standing-room-only crowd.

The problem with inorganic chemicals such as fertilizers, herbicides, and insecticides is that they cause nonpoint source pollution. That's the pollution that occurs when backyard watering, rainfall, and melting snow carry pollutants into underground drinking water, coastal waters, inland lakes, rivers, and wetlands. It is the leading cause of water pollution in America, and, unfortunately, it is an increasing problem. While the amount of chemicals used by agriculture has remained constant since 1979, the amount of herbicide in the form of weed-and-feed products used by homeowners has increased steadily. According to the Environmental Protection Agency, we currently use forty-nine million pounds each year. Admittedly, America has far more weekend gardeners who transform their lawns into emerald green deserts in order to battle dandelions, than rose exhibitors who spray Banner MAXX to control powdery mildew.

As Kitty says, it is possible to grow attractive, although not Queen-worthy, roses without chemicals. Old-garden roses, in particular, are often grown organically. Plants are fertilized with chopped banana peels; disease is prevented with a spray blend of baking soda and horticultural oil. These habits are commendable, although their use by lovers of antique roses is somewhat misleading. Many of the old varieties will die if sprayed with chemicals, so those who plant them often have no alternative to organics.

The perfection sought by exhibitors requires the use of chemicals. For Kitty, that means as few chemicals as possible. It is, she says with a sigh, "a delicate balance."

WE RECONVENE THE NEXT morning at 6:30 a.m. to spray the garden. It's a Sunday, with no rain or wind in the forecast. Kitty prefers to spray on Sunday mornings because most people are still asleep. "I don't want to spray when my neighbors are in their yards. And I want to be inconspicuous, which is hard to do in my outfit."

Kitty's spray clothes, which she lays out in the garage the night before, are indeed hard to miss. She suits up in zippered white Tyvek coveralls, black rubber boots, rubber gloves, and a shower cap. She used to wear a yellow plastic suit, which she says, "wasn't quite as scary to the neighbors." But the impermeable material proved too hot. "I just wish the Tyvek came in green. I'd blend into the yard." Kitty wears her own glasses instead of safety goggles, because the goggles steam up so badly that she can't see through them.

Still groggy without coffee, Bob has hauled the fourteen-gallon red Spray Boss off its charger and pulled it to the middle of the garage. Gray metal storage cabinets line one wall. A black florist's refrigerator in the far corner is full of slender show vases; Kitty will empty and turn it on just before she starts to cut stems for the show. Wheeled plastic trash bins by the refrigerator remind me of Clarence, although Kitty doesn't use them as planting containers; instead, she pulls them behind her as she deadheads. Ranged on the wall beside them are loppers, hedge shears, shovels, and rakes. "We're tool crazy," explains Bob as he returns from moving their van and car into the street.

He grabs a bucket and heads into the kitchen for warm water that he will pour into the sprayer; five buckets fill the machine to the halfway mark. As Kitty opens one of the cabinets, a sickly sweet odor wafts out. "Ick." She wrinkles up her face as she pulls out large plastic containers of Banner MAXX, a fungicide; Merit, an insecticide; and Indicate 5, a surfactant that helps chemicals spread better and last longer by neutralizing the pH of the water. Rosarians refer to such products as sticker/spreaders.

Kitty sets an old Hamilton Beach blender on a sheet of plywood supported by sawhorses. Most of this homemade table is populated by rose seedlings sprouting under grow lights, but she makes room for the chemicals and a large loose-leaf notebook. It contains the exhibitor's calendar, as well as the label of each product she uses pasted beside her handwritten notes on the correct measurements for her fourteen-gallon sprayer. "This way I know everything that I've ever done. I don't have to wonder, 'Did I spray Compass last time or not?' And I don't have to figure out mixing ratios at six thirty in the morning." She pats the book. "I have ten years of records in this thing."

Looking like a clean-room chemist in her white regalia, Kitty pours Banner MAXX, Merit, and Indicate 5, which is shocking pink, into the blender, secures the top, and pushes High. She lets the cherry liquid whirl for one minute, then pours it into the warm water in the sprayer tank. She stirs the concoction with an eighteen-inch-long dowel for a count of fifty and closes the unit.

After Bob snaps Kitty's mask into place, he disappears inside for coffee. Kitty switches on the Spray Boss, rolls it out of the garage, and trundles carefully down a small metal ramp that Bob has positioned over the front steps. She has twice lost control of the liquid-heavy sprayer in the ramp and splashed chemical mix over everything. "Never again," Kitty rolls her eyes with remembered horror.

KITTY HAD MENTIONED that several male exhibitors she knows don't wear protection when spraying. Cal Hayes, who'll be trying for his sixth Nicholson Trophy at the upcoming National, and San Diego exhibitor Jeff Stage, are two colleagues about whom she'd shaken her head. "I don't want to believe it, but they don't wear anything special!"

I could have told Kitty that Clarence Rhodes is another man who doesn't suit up to spray roses. Perhaps spraying without safeguards is a form of male bravado akin to leaving a seat belt unbuckled or riding a motorcycle without a helmet — *I am invincible. I do not need protection.* The day that I followed Clarence around, he wore his usual work khakis and a short-sleeved knit shirt.

Unsurprisingly, he began the process with a Secondary Products sprayer. "A good power-sprayer costs $300 to $500," he explained as he bent over a green board mounted with a six-inch-high pump, three-inch square switch box, rubber tube, PVC tube, and copper tube. "I figure that I can build one for $150." He tightened a Phillips head screw with a narrow flat-head screwdriver.

He spent seventy-five dollars on the pump. "It was such a bargain that I bought three of them." Thirty dollars for a chemical-ready plastic valve. The switch box came from a used industrial floor scrubber. I was so caught up in his creation that I forgot to ask how he acquired a used industrial floor scrubber.

"Most sprayers have twelve-volt batteries," he explained. "But being an engineer, I'm not big on batteries. This plugs in and will atomize the liquid at 100 psi [pounds per square inch]." He stood back, admiring his creation, which had the old-fashioned solidity of the best soapbox derby cars.

Clarence rinsed a white five-gallon bucket that was ringed, zebra-style, with black lines. "I make the lines with black permanent marker to indicate gallons. That way I don't have to measure. The only drawback is that you have to re-mark the lines every two or three years." He filled the bucket with cold water from an outdoor spigot.

Clarence poured fungicide and sticker/spreader into the water and swooshed the mixture around with his bare right hand. "I should have rubber gloves for this job, but after a lifetime . . ." A moue of consideration. "It's not good practice. But my body is large enough to absorb the minimal exposure and I always wash up afterward."

He stopped swooshing and walked over to the spigot where he did in fact wash thoroughly with water and Ivory soap. Then he slid the bucket onto the base of an upright mover's dolly, dropped in a short hose, plugged in an industrial-strength orange electrical cord, flipped a switch on the green motor board attached to the dolly's handles, and whrrr — as he depressed the handle on his homemade, forty-eight-inch, copper spray wand, a fine mist burst from the nozzle.

Clarence designed the spray wand with a nozzle that points upward to ensure that the blossoms are protected and undersides of leaves are adequately coated. Deftly, quickly, he darted the long slender wand in and out, in and out among leafy stems. Spray arched upward, coating the leaves. As the breeze blew, it drifted onto the neighbor's lawn. Clarence followed my gaze.

"His lawn's been in great shape ever since I put these roses out here. No weeds, no pests, no need to fertilize."

Before I could stop myself, I asked, "And no children or pets who play on the front lawn?"

A surprised laugh. "None of those either."

We have edged toward the sidewalk. "You stay here," commanded Clarence as he circled to the other side of the roses. "It's not dangerous, but you have to know what to do when the breeze is blowing at you."

I watched the green top of Clarence's baseball cap bob on the other side of the roses. Spray mist shimmered in the air. Suddenly, the spray clicked off and a rose cane bent toward me. "Here's the downy mildew problem." It was an unhappy sight. Dark, shriveled leaves, cane blotched with brown, pink blossoms faded and wrinkled.

"You can say what you want about spraying, but *look* at this." The cane wobbled as he pushed it with the tip of the spray nozzle. "Who'd want a garden like this? People who don't spray . . ." Instead of finishing his sentence, he appeared around the near side of the rose wall with the copper wand outstretched. The breeze had disappeared. "Give it a try."

The spray wand was surprisingly light, its length perfectly balanced by the weight of the hose screwed into the handle. I nudged the nozzle between roses and depressed the trigger. Swoosh! A satisfying spray mist rose and fell among the plants.

"After a while, you can do it fast. Stick it right in there. Move it about." He stood beside me, his right arm thrusting and parrying, simulating the desired in-vibrate-out movement. I tried to copy him and felt like an awkward ballerina beside George Balanchine. But I have to admit, it was fun — more than fun, actually, because it was purposeful. Puritan heritage strikes again.

Clarence unplugged the sprayer and we trailed around the far side of the garage toward the backyard. I carried the spray wand outstretched like an offering; I was terrified of banging the slender copper tube against the garage wall on one side and closely pruned junipers on the other. Clarence wheeled the spray cart behind me. "If I haven't used enough spray in front it splashes out of the bucket on this path." The cart rattled. "Looks good," he said.

We rounded onto a narrow brick path that bisects two wide beds of roses behind the garage and continued onto a small patio beyond. Clarence wheeled to a stop, plugged in the sprayer, and taking the wand from me, joggled it in his right hand, lips pursed in consideration. He resembled a chef testing the heft and balance of a new knife.

"So how important is all this?" he asked rhetorically, spray wand sweeping toward the zebra bucket on its moving dolly. "You need to keep your roses healthy." This was said firmly. "But you can get people so confused with measurements and time-tables and right way and wrong way that they stop growing roses." Clarence shook his head. "That's not good."

"It's terrible."

He nodded. "That's right. It *is* terrible, because . . . well . . ." He looked around. "See this rose?" He pulled a blossom toward us with the nozzle end of the spray wand. "That's 'Christopher Columbus'." Big, vibrant red-orange blooms glow against glossy, dark foliage. "Don't you just *love* that color?"

"I do."

"And smell that." He pointed to a tall hybrid tea with golden yellow blossoms. I inhaled. It smelled like ripe nectarines.

"So it's important, but not *so* important. The important thing is to grow roses. And if you don't want to spray, you can grow disease-resistant roses like floribundas and shrubs and stuff."

I burst out laughing. " 'Shrubs and stuff,' " I mimicked his tone of dismissal.

Clarence grinned. "As long as I don't have to grow them. Okay now, let's finish." He plugged in the unit. "Don't you think this thing works as well as a boughten sprayer?"

ADMITTEDLY, KITTY'S SPRAY BOSS functions as well as Clarence's Secondary Products creation. It wheels behind her like a medium-sized red pet. She uses the same up and down, in and out, back and forth movement that Clarence does. Mist drizzles over the hybrid teas and floribundas planted along the driveway and sidewalk. As she finishes each section, Kitty turns off the machine and remixes the ingredients with twelve turns of her stir stick. Twelve, not eleven. Kitty counts everything. Each large plant receives twelve seconds of spray; miniatures get five. The minis also receive five seconds of hand watering in cool weather, eight when it's hot. Hybrid teas get twenty seconds of water.

Panting slightly, she drags the still heavy Boss up her neighbor's driveway, threading her way through cars to reach the extra bed of floribundas. By the time she wends her way back down, two hands guiding the sprayer to keep it from hitting the vehicles, the canister is light enough that she can shake it to keep the mixture blended. Up the ramp and into the backyard. As Kitty sprays, she looks for problems. Today she sees only one dead cane that she will prune later. She forgets nothing; even the multitude of five-inch pots with seedlings regimented behind the pool receive five seconds of spray each. After an hour, she looks around the yard and, with a relieved shrug, mists the last of the chemical concoction on the lawn. "It keeps the grass free of rust," she explains. "And besides, I don't want to dump the solution in the street."

As she trundles the empty sprayer to the front driveway, she calls, "Okay! I'm done!" Bob is in charge of rinsing the machine with water and vinegar, and putting it back on the charger. Kitty strips off and heads inside to drink lots of water and take a long, hot shower. She wants to cleanse her system inside and out.

BOB LIKES ROSES because he likes his wife and he likes to grow things. He likes rose shows because, he says, "They're not just an old lady thing." As it turns out, the shows are filled with guys who are "pretty cool."

The competition thing, though? That's Kitty.

"I have always been very competitive. Spelling bees, writing contests, the drill team. At school I was shy around people, but I was not embarrassed about getting up during a spelling bee because I won all the time." She wins with roses, too, although her award display doesn't begin to rival Tommy and Luis's Ego Room. Like Rachel, Kitty only displays the "special things."

In the rose-patterned foyer between front and back hallways, she points to a group of plaques on the wall.

"This is an award for being an Outstanding Consulting Rosarian, of which I'm very proud."

Consulting rosarians — CRs for short — are the teachers of the rose world. Active ARS members who have grown roses for at least five years become CRs by attending a special ARS seminar and passing an exam. To remain in good standing, they must retake the seminar every four years and be willing to share their knowledge with anyone who needs advice. Want to figure out what's eating your rose buds before they open or identify a variety that you remember from childhood? Ask a consulting rosarian.

She points to an ARS President's Citation for her work on the *Rose Exhibitor's Forum,* an ARS quarterly publication devoted to all aspects of exhibiting. "And this is my certificate as president emeritus of the Los Angeles Rose Society." As she starts to walk back to the kitchen, she says, "We stack the rest of the plaques in a box."

"How about the crystal awards?" I ask.

"I keep the Waterford, but we give the rest of it away."

Bob chuckles as she says this. "Show Aurelia the closet."

"Oh, thank you, Bob." Kitty grimaces and leads the way into a guest room decorated with paintings of roses. "As I said, we donate most of it." She opens the door of a closet that is full almost to bursting with boxes marked CRYSTAL. She grins, unfazed. "I love to win." Then, as if to exonerate herself, she adds, "Wait until you talk to Jeff Stage. He *really* likes to win."

7

All for One and One for All

"Competitive? Oh yeah, with just about everything. When I first got into roses, I got me a garden log. Inside the cover I wrote: 'I love roses and I love the competition and I'm going to grow the best God damn roses I can.'" Jeff Stage grins — a thousand-watt, big-toothed smile set in a blizzard of beard.

Jeff is a retired navy sheet-metal mechanic who has been in roses since 1981. That was the year that he built a porch onto the side of his house in order to grow the Queen of Flowers. No, he didn't know much about them, but he liked to garden and had heard that roses did well in the San Diego climate. So he ordered eight or ten pretty ones from Jackson & Perkins, including a white hybrid tea named 'Honor'.

"I didn't know anything about growing them except that if you throw Bandini Rose Food at them and water 'em regular, they grow. I planted 'Honor' up under the eaves of the house and six weeks later it was so big that I couldn't see out of my picture window. I was feeding Bandini Rose Food every three weeks and the roses were trying to walk out of the yard.

"Anyway, I was sitting in the shop one day when this carpenter came by and said, 'What are you doing with that rose catálog?' I said, 'I've ordered some from this Jackson & Perkins place and they're doing real well.' He guessed that I'd bought 'Double Delight' because everybody was getting it then. Then I told him I had an 'Honor' that was over my head. He says, 'You're lying.' I said, 'I'll have my wife, Patty, take a picture of me standing in front of it.' I did and when I showed it to him, he said, 'Damn. You do grow 'Honor'.' I said, 'What's the big deal? It grows like a weed.' He said, 'I can't get mine past my knees.' As it turns out, he'd been growing roses for twenty-three years. Carl Mahaney. He became my first mentor."

Carl told Jeff to bring some blooms to the San Diego rose show.

"I hauled out every pot and pan in the house, filled them with water, put my roses in and loaded them into the back of my car. I was driving a Datsun 240z at the time. When I got there, roses and water had flopped all over." The 240z was a race-car look-alike with a high-rev engine and a tiny hatchback trunk — not rose friendly. Nonetheless, Jeff won two blue ribbons. "I said, 'Man, I can *do* this!'"

The following weekend, Carl and Jeff drove to a show in Arcadia. This time he won the Novice Trophy.

"That's when I knew that I wanted to exhibit roses. I wanted to compete. I went home and started digging. From the end of April until the first week of November, I dug an average of six hours a day. On weekends, I dug for ten or twelve hours a day. I dug up thirty yards of dirt, dumped it all into the canyon behind the house, replaced it with good loam and benches for pots."

When he wasn't digging, he read ten years worth of the American Rose Society magazine back issues.

"I would dig, read, go to work; dig, read, go to work."

"What did Patty say?"

"She thought I was nuts. She told her friends at work that I'd gone crazy on roses. They told her, 'Don't worry; it'll last a couple of years.' Isn't that sweet? *A couple of years!*" Jeff roars with laughter.

The miracle may be that Patty laughs, too.

Patty Stage is a slender, pale woman with a precise dark pageboy and a put-together style of dress. She has a welcoming nature and a smile as beautiful as her husband's. That husband is a tall bear of a man with aviator glasses and a sartorial preference for T-shirt, shorts, and flip-flops. They live in a brick and cream stucco ranch in a residential neighborhood near downtown San Diego.

Right now, Jeff grows fifty-five hybrid teas and eighty miniatures. The hybrid teas are planted in the ground in front of the house, along his driveway and along his neighbor's driveway. The neighbor, who teaches mathematics at San Diego City College, is reputed to have grown a wasteland until 1994, when Jeff took over the care of his yard.

"He comes over and says, 'It's amazing. I got grass and roses now!' We're real good friends."

The hybrid teas in the side-by-side yards are vibrantly healthy and the soil around them is even more weed-free than in Kitty's yard.

"That's because of you. I wanted to go to Kitty's rose society meeting last night, but no, we had to stay here and pull weeds because Aurelia was coming." Jeff grins wickedly. Patty reaches over and touches my arm.

"He's just giving you a hard time."

The miniatures are in a small backyard that is covered entirely
in decking. They are planted in containers set seven inches apart
in orderly rows on tiered, lattice-covered benches around the perimeter of the deck. I am reminded of class portraits from high
school — shortest students in front, tallest in the back.

"If I bring in a new one, something's got to go. It's that precise." Jeff leans in toward a 'Bee's Knees' to pinch off a side bud.
"What you do today saves work in May," he says when he notices
me watching. In addition to the ongoing work of disbudding, Jeff
is looking for basal breaks, or new stems, on the minis and hybrid
teas. More basal breaks mean more blossoms. Sometimes rosarians pinch off the top of a break when the stem is about twelve
inches long to encourage lateral growth. Lateral growth produces
even more blossoms, although the stems may be shorter and the
blossoms smaller. The decision to top the breaks depends on how
an exhibitor intends to use that particular variety — bouquet, for
example, or an attempt at Queen.

New green canes abound and Jeff has great plans for the ARS
Spring National. Like Rachel, he has set his sights on the Nicholson, although he tempers his ambition by saying, "Cal Hayes
is the best as well as being a great guy. He's won that Nicholson
more than anybody else and he wants to win it again." Jeff also
wants the Herb Swim, which requires five hybrid teas in separate
containers, and he plans to enter as many perfect hybrid teas as he
can in the horticultural specimen section of the show.

" 'Touch of Class'." He gestures toward a large, rather rangy
hybrid tea. "Amazing blossoms that change from coral orange to
pink, but it's never done much for me." The plant's inability to
bring home awards almost caused its downfall this winter. But
Jeff has heard that the Santa Clarita Rose Society has a new chal-

lenge class trophy that might suit it. He'll give the plant a year of reprieve. Next year, though, no win will produce a shovel.

Perhaps Jeff should model himself on Bob Martin, who uses his shovel to threaten before he digs. He maintains "the mother of all databases" on his show results. When he notices that a plant is underperforming, he gives it a warning. "The most subtle warning I have is to take a shovel and put it on the ground next to the rose. I leave it there for a day. The plant knows it's on probation. It's being watched."

"And it shapes up?"

"Yup. You'd be surprised by the results."

Jeff stops in front of 'Brandenburg Gate', the hybrid tea that grew well for Rachel Hunter in Kentucky but fares poorly in Temecula. He seems to concur with her judgment as he says, "In all my years of exhibiting, I've only gotten two of her blooms to a show." But those blooms won Queen and Princess at the 1998 Spring National in Albuquerque. Following Jeff's own rules, a two-bloom rose should have long-ago been pitched, but his bluff exterior hides a soft heart. "I think if you win Queen, you've earned your place in the garden." His eyes glisten ever so slightly.

Jeff almost didn't attend that 1998 Spring National, because cold weather slowed the bloom cycle of most of his roses. They flowered so late that he asked Patty to cancel his reservations. The next day he went outside to take one more depressed look at his plants.

"Late that afternoon, I started walking in with roses for the refrigerator. Patty watched me the first time and watched me the second time. The third time, she asks, 'What are you doing?'

" 'I'm cutting roses.'

" 'For what?'

" 'For the show.' "

" 'What show?' "

" 'The National in Albuquerque.' "

" 'I just canceled your room.' "

" 'Call them back!' "

Jeff drove for twelve hours in a frigidly air conditioned van with eighteen hybrid teas and eighteen minis. Fellow exhibitor Peter Alonso, whose own exhibition blooms had succumbed to bad weather, asked Jeff if he wanted help setting up his miniatures.

" 'Shit yes!' I jumped at the offer." For the next six hours, Peter groomed the miniatures, cooing over them in pleasure, while Jeff worked his hybrid teas.

"That 'Brandenburg Gate' had come up gorgeous. I knew it would be Queen of Show. My friends would walk by and I'd say, 'You want to see Queen?' " His white teeth gleam against his whiter beard as he laughs. "It drives them wild when you do that." This is called parading the Queen. It's standard practice among top male exhibitors, who use it as a way to show off and intimidate. I am reminded of Sun-tzu's *Art of War*: "Supreme excellence consists in breaking the enemy's resistance without fighting." It worked for Jeff. He won six trophies, including Queen of Show and Miniature Queen of Show.

While one can't imagine chess grandmaster Gary Kasparov helping rival Anatoly Karpov win a match against Boris Spassky, exhibitors often aid their competitors during shows. Sometimes an exhibitor without roses will work with an exhibitor who has roses, just as Peter assisted Jeff, but most often exhibitors simply are expected to offer honest advice when asked. In other words, if your biggest adversary asks you which of two 'Marilyn Monroe' hybrid teas is better, you are expected to tell him the truth.

This group-win approach to competition is so ingrained that when retired exhibitors Frank and Cherrie Grasso encouraged a no-assistance rule for the Southern California district several years ago, it nearly blew the local exhibiting community apart. The Grassos, who grew roses solely in order to exhibit them, believed that competition must be about what an exhibitor working alone can do with his or her own blooms. At one district show, Jeff circumvented the rule by offering detailed advice to Ron Gregory without touching Ron's blooms. Ron won a trophy. Those who agreed with the Grassos' rule were upset; others rallied for permission to help each other. The noncommitted hunkered down in their gardens and tried to stay out of the fray. Jeff grew so frustrated with the mudslinging that he gave his exhibiting equipment to Rachel Hunter and dug out twenty-five hybrid teas. Then the Grassos, who loved to exhibit, but did not like to garden, abandoned roses and retired to Ohio. The controversial regulation disappeared from the rule book. Jeff returned to exhibiting and giving advice. "To see someone smile after winning with something that you've helped them with, that's better than any personal trophy," he says. "Sometimes they come up to me years later and say, 'You remember that?' 'Yeah,' I tell them, 'I always remember.'"

Community-damaging feuds are so unusual that even four years after this most recent one, the pain of the misunderstanding has not disappeared. As a rule, competitors get along. While I like to believe that the harmony is due to the peaceable effect of the Queen of Flowers, it's more likely a result of the Queen's empty pockets. As I have mentioned, there is transitory glory, but no money, in showing roses. No one is battling for endorsement contracts or big purses. Everyone knows, says Bob Martin, that "the greatest rose in the show looks like squat the next day. One week, you're shut out; the next, you're Queen of Show. You can't hold enmity in that situation."

While exhibitors do not reap financial reward, some pursue rose show awards with an avidity that has won them the label "hardware hunters." Such exhibitors can never win enough silver-plated candlestick and crystal figurines to satisfy themselves. Joel Ross, a rose loving neurologist from San Diego says that hardware hunters spoil the pleasure for others. They don't understand that rose shows are fiercely competitive fun — Joel emphasizes *fun*. Instead, hardware hunters develop lists of awards and tick off their prizes with the unsociable ferocity of a grouse hunter out to bag the biggest count. They will be easy to spot at the Spring National, he says: they don't socialize, they're poor losers, and they're equally ungracious winners.

When it comes to spoiling the fun, some rosarians feel that exhibitors as a species have ruined rose societies. Exhibitors' enthusiasm means that often they shoulder most of the work involved in running a society. As I learned when I belonged to garden clubs, those who do the work in a membership organization set the calendar. Exhibitor-run societies often have more rose shows and more programs about exhibition varieties than nonexhibiting members would like. Like religious congregations divided on issues of doctrine, some afflicted rose societies have split into two — the church of the exhibitors and the church of the noncompetitive.

The California Coastal Rose Society, which Joel Ross helped establish, has taken a more healing approach. While the society organizes two large public shows a year, its monthly meetings are devoted to topics in which all rose lovers are interested. They accommodate both groups with an expanded program — the 7 p.m. meetings begin with a 6:30 session for Roseaholics, which is their term for exhibitors. During the session that I attended, a group of men and women aged twenty-five to eighty-something sat on the edge of their folding seats to review the value of triangulation when using three stems in an arrangement. They finished just as the room filled for the evening's main program, which included a spirited discussion about the value of horse manure as fertilizer. It was deemed excellent.

Jeff doesn't use horse manure, but he does like to garden. A fenced portico on one side of the house is a mass of orchids, staghorn ferns, and azaleas. It's a miniature jungle without a rose in sight.

"See this geranium? I collected it from a junk heap." The flower is an unusual deep orange. He shows off five cymbidium orchids, passed to him from exhibitors Lynn Snetsinger and Peter Alonso. "And this." He touches a pink orchid that arches toward us from a high shelf. "Isn't this pretty? I call it 'Grandmother's Orchid' because it bloomed on the day my grandmother died." He looks around his plant nursery. "I told you I like growing stuff. With the roses, though, it's different. I like growing them, but they are work. You can't just leave them alone to fend for themselves. You have to feed, spray, and prune." In fact, they are so much work that, like the Grassos, Jeff would not grow them without the reward of competition.

Jeff always starts to prune eight weeks before the first show, which means that he started four weeks ago. Three weeks ago, he began his intensive rose-care program. It looks like this:

	Feed	Spray
Week 1	Fish emulsion, Epsom salts 2 gallons per bush	Orthene, Compass, Funginex, Response
Week 2	Pentrex @ ½ strength 2 gallons per bush	Avid, Compass, Funginex, Response
Week 3	Gro-More 2 gallons per bush	Avid, Compass, Funginex, Response
Week 4	Gro-More 2 gallons per bush	Compass, Funginex, Response
Week 5	Pentrex @ ½ strength 2 gallons per bush Chelated iron/zinc	Avid, Compass, Funginex
Week 6	Fish emulsion, Epsom salts 2 gallons per bush	Orthene, Compass, Funginex
Week 7	Fish emulsion 2 gallons per bush	Avid, Compass, Funginex

As we review his preshow program, I'm struck by the order that exhibitors impose on their life in roses. Rachel begins to prune on a certain day; Kitty follows her rose-care calendar without deviation; Jeff sets his pots of minis seven inches apart on tiered benches. These habits bear no relation to the haphazard way most of us garden.

Opera singer Beverly Sills once said that she planned the minutest details of her professional life far in advance; she always knew five years in advance which role she would sing in what opera house.

"How confining!" exclaimed her interviewer.

"Not at all," said Sills. "I find it comforting."

An orderly approach to roses must also reassure. Donna Fuss looks forward to what will be accomplished each week of the sea-

son in the Elizabeth Park Rose Garden. And just as Sills anticipates what arias she'll be singing, Donna knows the schedule of
each year's rose shows months in advance.

This reminds me how much I like to record upcoming events
in my date book. Knowing that I've written them down reassures
me that I won't forget something important. But it also comforts
me on an emotional level. Whether it is a writing deadline or a
dinner party, scheduling events far ahead gives me a sense of purpose. I keep going in life partly because I promised to deliver an
article in three weeks or volunteer at the master gardener booth
two months from now; so must many methodical rosarians keep
going because the miniatures need deadheading and the floribundas need spraying. In the interests of full disclosure, I must admit
that it also makes me feel popular. Like a nineteenth-century girl
with a full dance card, I feel fashionable and a bit smug with a
tidy, inked-in calendar.

It's clear from Jeff's preshow schedule that exhibition roses are
prima donnas that grow best with labor-intensive care. But winning with even the most coddled blooms is so difficult that suddenly I wonder whether exhibitors cheat.

"Well yeah," says Jeff in a tone that implies I've been slow to
catch on. "I've heard that the people back east cheat."

"Just back east?" Now I'm the one who sounds bemused.

A sheepish grin. Exhibitors from every part of the country
cheat. Wires inserted into stems to make them straight, petals
removed from one rose and set into another to make the second
rose look more balanced, foliage glued onto stems, milk and oil
brushed onto foliage to make it glossy — it all happens, as does
willful damage to competitors' entries.

Sandy and Bob Lundberg are national exhibitors from South

Carolina. They are known for their exhibiting skill, manners in the midst of sleep-deprived competition, and for their generosity toward other rosarians. Unfortunately, that generosity hasn't protected them from cheaters. "It happens at the Nationals more often than local shows because the stakes are higher," says Sandy. "Bob and I once had roses stolen out of a challenge entry before it was judged. Lost the trophy because of it." She is certain she knows who damaged her entry, but she refuses to divulge the name of the malefactor, except to say, "You'd be shocked. One of the most famous names in the rose world today. You have certainly met *that* person."

When Sandy encountered the cheater near one of her entries the following year, she "went all fluttery and helpless." She pretended that she was too nervous to confirm the number of blooms in what should have been a bowl of twenty. The alleged thief agreed to count them with her. "So I knew that entry, at least, was safe. But Bob and I stood by our other challenge entries until all the exhibitors had to leave the room." Her gentle Virginia accent hardens. "You just have to learn who you can trust and who you can't."

Many rose varieties resemble each other, which can lead to temptation for some exhibitors and confusion for others. When you need six specimens of one variety and you only have five, for example, it is tempting to substitute a similar bloom and hope that the judges don't spot the difference. Do it more than once at one show and you are probably cheating. Jeff caught an exhibitor substituting a white hybrid tea named 'Anastasia' for a white hybrid tea named 'Crystalline' three times at one local show.

Misname a rose once and berate yourself afterward, and you have probably made an honest mistake. Jeff won Queen at a San

Diego Rose Show with a beautiful 'Silverado' that he labeled as 'Paradise'.

"To this day I have to live with that." Jeff doesn't even grow 'Paradise'. "What was I thinking?" He slaps his forehead. "I heard that the judges almost came to blows over it. The chair of judges picked it up and put it next to the other Silverados to prove that it wasn't 'Paradise'." Jeff's reputation for honesty won him the trophy and permanent embarrassment. "Other exhibitors are always going to jab me up because I won with a misnamed rose."

Speaking of trophies, the Stages have hung a few special plaques on the wall and put the Waterford in a three-shelf hutch in the dining room. Patty switches on the hutch's interior light, making crystal vases, bowls, and small covered boxes sparkle.

"For a while we had trophies everywhere," she says. "In the closet, under the bed. We had trophies in boxes in the garage."

"It was getting crazy," agrees Jeff. "So one day we hauled out 99 percent of the crystal and put in on tables in the driveway for passersby to take. 'Take whatever you want,' I told them. After dinner, there were these two ladies walking on the other side of the street. I called out, 'You guys want some crystal?' They said, 'Sorry, sir, we don't do drugs.' 'No, no, not meth,' I said. 'Glassware!'" He cracks up. Patty starts to laugh. That makes Jeff laugh so hard that he has to pull out a big white handkerchief to wipe his eyes. He sighs. "Anyway. The ladies did come over and then they went to get their friends. That's how we got rid of our crystal. Except the Waterford, of course."

The laughter vanishes as swiftly as it came. Hands on hips, Jeff eyes the twinkling shelves. In four weeks, he plans to win another sparkler.

8

What We Do for Love

 If you ask Dr. Satish Prabhu when he starts to plan for a show, he says, "Two years before. You must select and plant roses for a show two years in advance." In six days, he will know if his two-year-old choices for the Spring National were correct.

Satish and his wife, Vijaya, live in South Carolina, which along with the other southern mid-Atlantic states, boasts a temperate rose-growing climate that nourishes a large community of national exhibitors. The Prabhus' close friends, Sandy and Bob Lundberg, live nearby, as do the coinventors of the nationally famous bloom protector, Dennis and Suzy Bridges and Fred and Jack Wright. For a while, these exhibitors' gracious southern manners lulled me into believing that they were less driven than their western competitors. Then Satish mentioned that Fred checks the temperature of his rose transportation cooler every hour when traveling. "For sure I do," said Fred when he showed me his technique for protecting early growth on 'Color Magic', a tender hybrid tea — he slips PVC tubes over each new cane in late winter. It's a labor-intensive process that only an exhibitor could love, but Fred cared solely for the anticipated result. With a grin as wide and seductive as the Big Bad Wolf's, he said, "Come next season, I plan to kick butt with these 'Magics'."

Ideally, he would love to kick California butts. Exhibitors from different parts of the country admire and detest each other in almost equal measure. Theirs is a generalized prejudice that permits Jeff Stage to disparage roses that win in the East as "tulips on thorny stems" in the same conversation that he describes visiting his "good buddy" John Mattia, who lives in Connecticut. Eastern exhibitors tend to believe that western exhibitors show imperfect blooms that are so large they look as if they're on steroids. Westerners accuse easterners of growing "buds," or what Jeff calls tulips. Southerners say that the North exhibits unopened blooms. Northerners assert that exhibitors from temperate climes are wimps who have no idea how hard it is to run out before the first hard frost and put covers on four hundred plants. Warm-weather gardeners are liable to respond, "And what kind of idiot grows roses that far north anyway?" which only inflames the rivalry.

Satish is a courteous man who does not express his opinions quite so bluntly. Yet he anticipates the upcoming National with such keenness that energy seems to radiate from his small, slender frame. He tends his roses in a large, classically beautiful garden behind the house. The garden surrounds a square of emerald grass decorated with a stone fountain. The twelve fifty-foot beds around the fountain hold about 350 hybrid teas, floribundas, and miniatures mulched with pine needles. They are perfectly cared-for plants with spotless foliage, organized by type — two beds of miniatures, two of floribundas, three beds of AARS winners, and so forth.

Although exquisite, the blooms are not nearly as large as they should be by now. Satish is worried that a cold South Carolina spring will keep him from taking much at all to the National. He's determined to push enough hybrid teas into bloom to mount a fight for the Nicholson, though, and there will probably be enough mini-floras to try for the J. B. Williams Trophy.

"They do look beautiful," I offer.

"Thank you." He nods, punctilious. "But how well your roses look at home is immaterial. They have to be the best roses on the show table when the judges pass by. Exhibitors will look at the Queen-winning bloom and say, 'But I had a rose that was much better last week in my garden.' They are telling the truth, but it doesn't matter. It also doesn't matter when you have roses too young to take to a show" — he gestures around the garden — "that look perfect when you return home. They sit there laughing at you — the Monday Queens."

Satish takes vacations from his anesthesiology practice prior to ARS Nationals. One week to prune, another week later in the season for "catch-up," and finally, a week just before the show — *this week* — to protect the most promising blossoms. It looks as if a mad scientist is trying to punish recalcitrant blooms by imprisoning them in big jugs. Satish protects his show-worthy flowers by covering them with damaged five-gallon water bottles that a local bottling plant gives him for free. He describes the bottles, which are huge compared with the Bridges/Wright Bloom Protector, as "the mother of all protection." His dark eyes sparkle as he says this.

Four oval beds of antique and David Austin roses color the outer edge of the yard; they look as vibrant as the modern hybrids around the fountain. We inhale the spicy scent of *Rosa rugosa* var. *alba* and pink 'Crested Moss', whose fringed and mossy sepals project from the buds to resemble the French tricorne hat made famous by Napoleon.

"Old-garden roses have a beauty of their own," says Satish. "Any complete rose garden should include them; they are where roses started." Despite his affection for them, Satish won't take any of his old roses to the National. May 8 is far too early for flowers that bloom in June.

Satish's belief that complete rose gardens should include antique varieties is rather like stipulating that every family gathering include grandmothers. Despite knowing firsthand that grandmothers and teenagers do not always mix well, I find myself agreeing with him. Although, I must say that modern hybrids do dazzle. Perusing the glossy full-color pages of rose catalogs is as painfully tempting as walking into Catherine's Chocolates, my favorite candy store in Massachusetts. Just as I long to purchase every dark-chocolate-covered dried fruit that Catherine makes — unctuous, spicy candied ginger is beyond description — I can succumb to fifteen roses in the new J&P catalog without thinking. How can one resist apricot 'Gold Medal', or 'Black Magic', whose "black buds slowly unfold to spellbinding, dark garnet flowers"?

Yet, as much as I like to look at modern hybrids, I love to inhale old varieties. As Shakespeare wrote, "The rose looks fair, but fairer we it deem, for that sweet odour which doth in it live." It is difficult to breed flowers for more than one or two variables at a time, so the quest for disease resistance, Technicolor, and perfect, urn-shaped blossoms has forced scent into the background in the past forty years. Keith Zary may want to select for aroma, but for a commercial breeder the choice between a scented pretty rose and an unscented showstopper is no choice at all. Old roses almost always smell like — well, like your grandmother's rose perfume — nose-tinglingly full and sweet. Rose oil is said to arouse desire while it calms the nerves. No wonder essential oil of antique damask roses remains a major perfume ingredient.

The flower forms of old-garden roses vary more than those of the newer plants; they offer everything from the simple five-petal *R. canina,* whose blossoms look like those of its rose relative, the apple, to the great pouf of *R. centifolia.* And the shape of the plants themselves, while not as pristine as new hybrids, often has a pleasingly abundant look. Admittedly, some might describe their growth habit as uncontrollable; instead, they remind me of gorgeous French film stars of a certain age, all the more interesting because they are no longer young. Old-garden roses and mature women have stories to tell, knowledge to share. Think of Jeanne Moreau or Catherine Deneuve — such beauty, such experience. Even better, think of Josephine Bonaparte, the beautiful commoner from Martinique who captured the heart of a younger man and saved hundreds of roses — antique roses — from extinction.

Regardless of the antiques in his garden, his is not a *real* rose garden, says Satish. It is an exhibitor's collection planted with lots of multiples and persnickety show blooms. But anyone willing to work even a little bit can have a real rose garden.

"If someone asks me how to grow roses, I tell them one thing straight away. You cannot have a rose garden simply because you want to. You must enjoy the work of growing roses. If you ignore them they are like your teeth. They will go away." Satish loves to make such quips; in his musical, precise voice, he inserts them wherever he can in a conversation.

The average gardener should decide ahead of time which they want, advises Satish: a reasonable rose garden, a very good rose garden, an exhibitor's rose garden. "Each of them is exponentially more work, but for any of them you need five things." He ticks off the requirements on lean fingers. "Number one: Site. Stay away from trees and buildings. Number two: Soil. It must drain well. Number three: Water. You need to water enough and regularly. Number four: Spray — for disease in particular." Satish has always lived in hot, humid, disease-producing places. "Number five: Fertilizer. Roses are hungry." Now that he owns a "huge monster sprayer" it only takes three hours to fertilize and one hour to spray his garden.

Satish's wife, Vijaya, says that he intimidates people with all this advice. Gardeners ask how to care for their few roses and Satish can't help but educate them thoroughly.

"You need to tell them just what they need to know at the time, not overwhelm them." Vijaya's hand rests on Satish's shoulder to gentle the admonition.

"But if I do that they come back and say that their roses don't look like my roses. They think I'm keeping secrets!"

"*Then* you tell them about the extra care needed to grow show roses."

"But — " He believes that the more information, the better; knowledge is power.

Satish may plant and tend the roses, but Vijaya cuts them for the show. In fact, she does all the preshow preparation — fills out labels, stocks the tool kit, buys ice, readies the boxes, cuts and packs the blooms. As William Carlos Williams wrote, "It is at the edge of the petal that love waits." How true, smiles Vijaya. Satish won her heart with roses.

HE HAD LOST his own to the flower years before. As a child in India, Satish copied his neighbors and began to grow roses in front of his family's rented house. He was so captivated by the challenge and the glorious results that when he went off to medical school, he persuaded others to supply his passion.

"I had no garden, but my professors, who lived along the main street, had gardens and gardeners. They grew everything except roses. So I asked, 'Would you like to grow roses?' They said, 'Isn't it tough?' 'No!' I promised. 'I'll tell the gardeners what to do.' Within twelve months, all those people had more than four hundred roses each."

Satish was allowed to pick them whenever he wished. He began his harvest when he met Vijaya.

"She was number two in her class of thirty thousand at university. And she was a really popular girl. The cricket players and football players were all after her. I used to take her lots of roses. Lots and lots of roses! When she finally married me, all those athletes said, 'Why did she choose you?'" He laughs and shakes his head. Graceful Vijaya appears quietly behind him; pats his shoulder; settles on a nearby couch.

"I said, 'You'll never know!'" He removes his glasses, revealing large dark eyes fringed with long lashes. "You know what I didn't know? Vijaya loved roses. I took them to her because it was all I had to give, but she had always loved them. They were the perfect gift."

When Satish and Vijaya moved from India to America, they lived in an apartment.

"No roses." Satish's hands open wide, palms up. Thirty years later, he still sounds desperate. "I actually went out and bought packaged roses from Kmart, hoping that I'd find a home for them in one of my professor's gardens just like I did in India." He shakes his head. "I asked colleagues if they would give me a corner of their yard where I could plant a rose garden.

" 'Why would you do that?'

" 'Because I love to grow roses.'

" 'What would I have to do?'

" 'Nothing.'

" 'Who will buy them?'

" 'I will. I'll do the whole thing.' "

Again, he shakes his head. "They refused, so I said to Vijaya, 'We've got to buy a house.' "

In 1979 they moved to Columbia, South Carolina, for Satish's medical residency and told their real estate agent to find them a house with big windows overlooking a flat backyard with few trees. Then they ordered the entire Jackson & Perkins rose catalog.

"Cover to cover," says Satish. "Everything in it. 'Collection of three' — I ordered that. 'Collection of five' — I ordered that, too."

"He had been without roses for so long," explains Vijaya. "We had the space and could finally afford it, so that's what happened."

Satish nods. "I was hungry for roses." His solemn face suddenly beams. "Do you know, we got a call from the manager of the J&P Sales Department. She thought we were a commercial establishment!"

MAINE ROSARIAN SARI HOU says that there is a sad story behind every rose garden, and that sadness becomes happiness in that garden. That was certainly true for Charles Chapin, the twentieth-century newspaper editor imprisoned in Sing Sing for killing his wife. Struggling with despair — "I believed I would die or go crazy before long" — Chapin convinced the warden to appoint him prison horticulturalist. After building a garden of spring bulbs and evergreens, he contacted the American Rose Society. "A rose bush with a hundred blooms on it would look like a million dollars to my famished, rose-hungry eyes." When ARS president J. Horace McFarland published Chapin's plans in the 1923 Annual, members inundated Chapin with plants. Within a year, thousands of roses bloomed on the grounds of Sing Sing. They attracted visiting garden clubs as they saved Chapin's sanity. "I do not claim that flowers reform men, nor that the gardens or the roses reformed Chapin," wrote the prison warden in later years. "But they gave him a new perspective." Chapin, who became known as the Rose Man of Sing Sing, said, "The greatest joy I had known during the years I had been in prison was when I saw the lovely blooms."

In the Western world, roses and love have intertwined since the ancient Greeks designated *R. damascena* sacred to Aphrodite, goddess of love. When I order damask rose tincture from Artemis Herbs in England, it arrives with the notation that roses have a "particular place for comforting those who have been bereaved or find it hard to love themselves." Smelling the tincture or taking a couple of drops on the tongue evidently offers an immediate sense of well-being and calm. Two drops — it tastes sweet and astringent — did produce a sense of serenity, although that may have been the power of suggestion.

Passions — be they love affairs or hobbies — are notoriously demanding. Oscar Wilde wrote, "If you want a red rose . . . you must build it out of music by moonlight, and stain it with your own heart's-blood." When a rose obsession flowers, someone must accommodate or sacrifice. Remember Frank Benardella's wife, June — "Mountains this year, or rose convention? Seashore or rose convention? The rose convention always wins." Rather than lose a husband and father to roses, June Benardella accommodated Frank's new love by transforming rose conventions into family vacations. The mistress, in effect, became a friend of the family.

Cal Hayes's wife, Barb, too, co-opted the mistress. The day that Cal went out to buy a few miniature roses and came home with fifty, she decided that if she wanted to stay married, she needed to learn a little something about roses. She doesn't do anything in the garden except admire. But she, too, has transformed rose shows into family vacations, and, as Patty Stage does for Jeff, Barb develops Cal's preshow checklist and organizes his equipment.

Chi Ning Liu, husband of Cynthia Chuang, a California rose arrangement exhibitor, has sacrificed his position in the family hierarchy owing to roses.

"In China, husband should be number one. But for Cynthia, I am number four behind roses, camellias, and children." He says this with a smile, explaining that grandchildren will one day drop him to number five. Rose exhibitors are "crazy," he adds with a

shake of his head. "But I join her in the craziness. I have started
to paint pictures of roses."

Mike McCarthy, who is married to northern California exhibitor, Susan Chan McCarthy, accommodates her rose affair with a
live-and-let-live attitude. He likes their rose-inundated home and
admires Susan's success. During show season, he says, "I mostly
help by staying out of her way." As it turns out, this is easy. Rose
show season coincides with baseball season. He watches. She
prunes. It works.

ARS president Steve Jones's first wife wasn't as accommodat-
ing. Steve had lost his heart to roses as a child because his grandmother's name was Rose and his mother's middle name is Rose.
Really, that is how he explains his passion. He says that he had no
choice when he bought a house in Valencia in 1984. It would be
landscaped in roses.

"So, being a rather compulsive person, I went down to the local nursery, bought every rose book I could find, and read the hell
out of them."

After cross-referencing all the rose characteristics that he
wanted — award winning, certain colors, fragrance — Steve developed a list of twelve varieties and repaired to local nurseries
where he found only five of the twelve.

"So I went with plan B, which was to note what the nurseries
had and look them all up." He selected seven more varieties to
fulfill the desired twelve, but somehow failed to look up height,
growth pattern, and disease resistance.

"Right on the street, I put 'Queen Elizabeth', a fragrant pink
floribunda that grew very tall and took over the sidewalk, so that
no one could walk by. Next to it, I put this dinky little floribunda

that grew to three feet. Then a couple of medium-sized shrubs and a spreading one that grew through everything else. It was quite a mess."

Steve decided to join the American Rose Society. Under the tutelage of the ARS magazine *American Rose,* he began to buy the right types and plant them correctly. He also began to attend rose shows. At a show in Arcadia, California, he was persuaded to join the Pacific Rose Society. "And that was that."

Not as far as his wife was concerned. When he said that he wanted to exhibit rose arrangements, she told him that he had no talent.

"I went out and got all the books I could find on arranging and then I started winning. I proved her wrong."

When he decided to become an arrangement judge, she said, "There's no way on earth you can be an arrangement judge." At least, that's what Steve says that she said. He went to the ARS school for arrangement judges. "Not only did I pass, I was the first person ever to score 100 percent on the written exam and the practicum where you point-score four arrangements. Needless to say, I just slapped that certificate down on the table in front of my wife." It was about then that his then-wife became his ex-wife.

BOB MARTIN ALSO FOUND sorrow in his rose garden before he found happiness. The man whose book *Showing Good Roses* has made him famous in the exhibiting community, began his love affair with the Queen of Flowers at age thirteen. That's when he inherited his older brother's job of hawking flowers on Los Angeles street corners. He sold just about everything, but roses were his favorite. So, in 1971, when his wife asked him to plant a rose garden beside their new house in Irvine, Bob said, "Well, okay. I like roses." Bob has a deadpan delivery reminiscent of Raymond Chandler's detective Philip Marlowe.

Bob joined the American Rose Society to learn how to tend them. Then they moved to Pasadena. His wife suggested a new rose garden, and on Valentine's Day 1980 he planted climbers, antiques, and hybrid teas. In 1985 they moved again. This house had a huge yard. His wife envisioned a sixty-rose garden. Bob filled it with four hundred, because, he says, "Roses are the most beautiful plants there are."

They moved once more, and again Bob built a four-hundred-specimen rose garden. That's when he got divorced.

It wasn't the roses as much as it was the rose shows. Bob began to show roses in 1986 after being fascinated by a presentation on exhibiting at the Pasadena Rose Society. He won his first Novice Trophy in 1988, bringing his young son along to carry in their entry. Showing led to judging. Judging led to becoming chair of the ARS Horticultural Exhibitor's Committee, and editor of its quarterly publication, *Rose Exhibitor's Forum*. All the while, he maintained a successful law practice.

"I love the practice of law, but it is so intense. Before roses, I'd come home and my mind would wander back to work. I lay awake at night and thought about work. I needed a hobby that I could be as excited about as I was about law. Going into the rose garden is like throwing a switch. All I think about is the roses. Psychologists say that kind of shift is a good thing."

But not all wives or children feel the same way. Bob reports that his now-grown children, even the son who helped win that first Novice Trophy, don't like his "rose habit."

"They say it's an unhealthy passion." Frustration rasps his

voice. "How roses could be a bad thing totally, absolutely, utterly escapes me."

Then, at a rose society banquet, Bob met a woman who shares his obsession. "It wasn't a love-at-first-sight, steamy rose affair," says Bob about his wooing and winning of Dona. "We were two people passionate about roses who found each other and fell in love."

Now he lives in Arizona with Dona and 380 roses. Being married to a woman who once grew over 450 varieties of hybrid tea, floribundas, miniatures, and old-garden roses is a dream come true for Bob. However, he says, "It's got its moments."

"The one thing about doing roses by myself is that I could do everything exactly the way I wanted. Now I've got another opinion, and the problem is that it is a good opinion with a knowledge of roses that is equal to mine. So, you know, we've gotten into a couple of them. I actually told her that her approach to watering was wrong. She's lived in Arizona for years, so I can't believe I said that. Anyway, the first year in 'our' garden, I watered a bunch of roses and killed them. Dona just smiled — she's got the most beautiful smile you've ever seen."

ARS PRESIDENT STEVE JONES also found new love with a woman who admires his roses and shares his enthusiasm for collecting. Steve could fairly be termed a compulsive collector. He collects roses, rose-related books, rose journals, and esoteric information about gravestone rose decorations, which he trolls cemeteries to photograph. He owns a full set of the *British Royal National Rose Journal* and a full set of the ARS magazine *American Rose*. He also has a complete collection of the New Zealand/

Australian rose society journal published when the countries'
rose societies functioned as one.

"And I have a few Canadian and Indian rose annuals as well."

Steve has a need to possess, certainly, but he also collects in order to learn. He has read every English-language rose book in his
collection, which is one of the largest in the United States. When
the book is written in another language, he strives to translate
as much as he can, working back and forth, for example, with
French-English or German-English dictionaries.

He pulls a little leather-bound volume in a dark slipcase off
a top shelf to show me — *Les Roses*, published in 1814. He leafs
cautiously to a stiffened page that is bright with the image of a
pink damask.

"See this? These are hand-painted originals. Thieves rip pictures like these out of antique books. Wish I could afford to save
them all."

As president, Steve is trying to promote the society among
people who live in gardenless apartments or who have grown too
old to garden.

"Just because you don't have any roses doesn't mean that you
don't like them anymore," he brandishes the antique book to
make his point. Reading about roses, discussing roses, looking at
pictures of them, inhaling them — there is no reason to stop doing any of that. Indeed, on days when others are battling mildew
and weeds, the gardenless rose society member may be the happi-
est rose person of all.

Steve and Sue's living room and den are adorned with rose
images, including one of John Mattia's rose-inspired digital photographs. The guest bathroom, similar to most rosarians' guest

bathrooms, has rose-patterned shower curtain, tissue box, and floor tile.

"Anything rosy, I collect," explains Steve.

Steve and Sue have other collections. They own so many Department 56 miniature village scenes that the weight and number of the pieces recently threatened to overwhelm the attic. At Christmastime, the entire house becomes a stage set for the collection; preparations are so extensive that Sue and Steve begin to plan Christmas in September.

They collect porcelain dolls and Boyds Bears.

"He started on Boyds; then I took over." Sue opens her eyes wide in mock innocence.

"We're both collectors and that's dangerous," says Steve.

Sue nods. "We're a little nuts." As we speak, she clicks her computer mouse, researching current Boyds Bear prices on eBay. "We're best friends with Doug the UPS man."

Steve and Sue also collect wine, which is stored in a large closet in the library. Actually, the wine collection has jostled out into the library proper where it blocks access to foreign rose encyclopedias. Steve makes a "wild guess" that they own over five hundred bottles. He and Sue know every Santa Barbara vintner depicted in the movie *Sideways*.

"We have a little bit of everything, although we favor wine that is heavy on flavor. I've discovered that a lot of the wines I like are created by women winemakers." As he shifts a bottle of pinot noir to reach a two-book Swedish set on roses — "The only problem is that I have to take them to a Swedish colleague to translate the text" — a book about snakes tumbles off the shelf. Steve picks it up, dusts it off, considers it for a moment before looking up. He looks serious.

"Herpetology was a former hobby. Rattlesnakes, now there's an interesting subject." Before I can decide how to respond, he grins. "Back to roses, the most interesting subject of all."

Steve will be a judge at the upcoming National. He warns me that between watching exhibitors and waiting for the results, I'll get no sleep. "You'll love it," he promises.

9

It's Showtime

Prelude — 3:00 a.m. to 9:30 a.m.
Exhibitors and arrangers can work
in the rose show prep area.

"I'm looking for a rose with a center, but I can't find shit." Cal Hayes is bent low over the third crate from the left in a row of ten red plastic milk crates lined up on the beige-carpeted floor.

The milk crates are packed with a garden's worth of long-stemmed roses in cut-down quart cartons labeled ALBERTSON'S 2½% MILK. Pink, blush, apricot, ruby, scarlet, peach, carmine. Cal flicks them, rustles them, pulls a hot pink bloom from the mass and drops it back into its container with a grunt.

"Sixty God damn blooms and not a winner among 'em." He stands and stretches, a trim figure in blue. Denim shirt tucked into jeans. Tooled leather belt with a large silver buckle. White sneakers. White hair brushed back from his forehead. Blue eyes behind silver-frame glasses. He reaches abruptly past me and pulls a blush pink bloom from the number-four milk crate. "Glad I saw that." He pokes the stem into a narrow tube vase and sets it beside eleven roses in identical containers ranged on a twelve-foot folding work table.

"Cold, cold, it's so cold!" Kitty trots by. She is wearing a fuchsia tracksuit and carrying a pink and powder blue plastic makeup case. She sets the case on a distant table with an audible clunk and bustles back toward us. Bob appears carrying a black plastic milk crate filled with floribunda roses. He's dressed in blue corduroy shorts and a Hawaiian shirt. As usual, he is barefoot.

"For this you get me out of bed at two thirty in the God damn morning. No coffee, no breakfast. I should drop this thing right here. Mornin,' Cal. See you've got a table of losers there."

"Losers, Bob," Cal answers without looking up. He is maneuvering a Q-tip between the petals of a carmine-colored hybrid tea that already bristles with six Q-tips.

Kitty's curls snap with energy. "Bob, it's 3:33."

Bob heads out into the predawn darkness through the open double doors at the back of the ballroom. He needs to get fifty more floribunda sprays and thirty miniatures.

At 3:35 a.m. the Silver Ballroom at the Town and Country Resort Hotel in San Diego, aka the prep room for the ARS Spring National Rose Show, buzzes with frantic purpose. People carry bins of miniatures and wheel floribunda-filled trolleys that resemble miniature rose parade floats through the massive, high-ceilinged ballroom that is packed with twelve-foot rectangular tables and six-foot diameter circular tables. They lug plastic buckets of water from a sink in a corner room to their tables, which are invisible beneath blooms and the test-tube style vases provided by the organizers. Men hug men, women hug women, men and women hug. While they embrace, they peer over each other's shoulders to examine their competitor's entries.

The walls of the room are papered in silver and white tracery. The woodwork is painted white. Every fluorescent light ranged across the high ceiling is turned on. The total effect is an eye-straining dazzle.

I shiver in the air-conditioned chill, but many competitors have a slight dew of sweat along the hairline. They began to arrive at 2:50 a.m., most of them in vans in which the rear seats have been temporarily replaced by crates of roses and rose-grooming paraphernalia. Competitors who flew arrived yesterday. There is a walk-in cooler available, but most have kept their roses in their rooms with the air conditioning cranked. Few have slept. But with just under six hours to go before the show opens for judging at 9:30 a.m., no one is yawning.

"Ron! You gonna win this year?" Jeff Stage greets a man whose hybrid teas already stand rigid in their vases on a neighboring table. It is Ron Gregory, the exhibitor who won an award several years ago with Jeff's hands-off assistance.

"I am Jeff, I am."

"Like hell you are. That Herb Swim Trophy is mine, damn it." Jeff slaps him on the back. Ron reels slightly.

Jeff is in green shorts, a hooded blue sweatshirt and flip-flops. Ron is in wrinkled beige pants and an untucked lightweight cream shirt of the sort that Philippine dictators made popular. He gives the impression of hiding shyly behind his gold-rimmed aviator-style glasses.

"Jeff is one of the best exhibitors in the country. You do know that?" I nod. Ron whispers and with the growing hum of voices in the increasingly crowded room, I have to lean almost forehead to forehead to hear him. He starts to speak again, but Jeff calls, "Your roses, Ron." Ron breaks off midsentence to return to his corner of the table.

Jeff stands behind a pale cream hybrid tea named 'Crystalline', one of the eighty-five roses he brought to the show. "She's a tough little competitor," he comments as he pulls down one petal and inserts a Q-tip into the opening between petals. When he lets go, the Q-tip remains secure, pointing out from the blossom.

"The Q-tip is your most important tool. It acts as a lever, see?" He slides another Q-tip between two pale petals that lie flat against each other. "This holds the petals flexed outward into a perfect circle. In fact, you want to take the petal past the ideal, then hope against hope that when you take the Q-tips out, the petals stay where they're supposed to."

He picks up a pair of deckle-edged shears and trims about one-sixteenth of an inch from the edge of a leaf. The result looks entirely natural. He hands me the leaf sliver to inspect. The pointy tips of its irregular edge are tinged brown. "Wind damage. Competitors can remove anything they want from a rose, but they cannot add anything." He yawns. It is 4 a.m.

"Have you slept?"

"Four hours."

He moves to a deep red blossom, and with a miniscule wood-handled knife that is almost invisible in his large hand, trims a blind — or flowerless — shoot that he had missed in the garden. His glasses slip down his nose as he trims. "This knife was given to me by a friend who thought it was funny that a guy as big and ugly as me liked roses. So he gave me this tiny knife." He glances up. "Here comes the ministering angel."

Patty appears holding two steaming paper cups of coffee that will be their only breakfast until the show closes for judging. Jeff grooms better on an empty stomach. In blue slacks and matching jacket, perfect makeup, hair combed, Patty might be setting off for a ladies luncheon. Jeff gestures toward a cluster of hybrid teas in vases on the other side of the table.

"These are all to be washed."

Patty's smile transforms into a wry moue. "Swell. I just love washing foliage at four in the morning." She takes a sip of coffee, puts down her cup and sets to work. She works leaf by leaf, supporting each one from below with her left hand as she wipes it with a damp cloth held in her right hand.

"Jeff?" Ron appears at Jeff's shoulder holding a pale hybrid tea in a vase. Jeff peers down into the center of the rose.

"Okay. Here's what you do." He takes a narrow artist's brush from its resting place behind his ear. "Put the back end of a paintbrush into the rose." He looks up and grins. "I have several different sizes of back ends, so to speak." He inserts the tip of the slender handle, which is no more than one-eighth inch in diameter, between two petals. As he begins to move the handle concentrically away from the center of the blossom, petals flutter and settle into the desired spiral.

"Ahh," murmurs Ron.

Jeff removes the artist's brush. Both men gaze at the flower.

Mournfully, Ron says, "The petals are perfect now. But by nine thirty, the center will be too open." Jeff nods.

"Just to break your heart."

Ron wanders back to his table. Jeff picks up a Q-tip and pokes it between the petals of a crimson blossom.

"I'm taking the Nicholson Bowl from Cal this year," he glances toward Cal Hayes, four tables away.

The Nicholson Perpetual Challenge demands nine perfect, long-stemmed hybrid teas, each a different variety, displayed in individual vases. We look over at Cal, who stands at his table be-hind a row of fourteen Q-tip-bristling hybrid teas rigid in test-tube vases. Unlike every other table in the room, Cal's table holds only the flowers he is grooming. All the rest of his stock is in those ten crates on the floor.

"Actually, Jeff, I think that I will try for the Nicholson this year." Ron has returned. As he speaks, he drops his head and seems to be talking to his shirt pocket.

"Damn Ron, that's great! Let's see what you have."

The Nicholson Perpetual Challenge Bowl is just that — a bowl. Admittedly, it is more of a bowl than most of us need. Eigh-teen inches in diameter, silver, embossed around the rim with stylized roses, set atop a three-layer wedding-cake style silver and mahogany stand. It comes with an oak and brass plaque on which each winner's name is engraved. In between Spring Nationals, the bowl generally stays in the ARS vault as winners must pay for insurance and shipping if they want to take it home for the year.

SIX HUNDRED GARDENERS are vying for the awards at the Spring National this year. Like every ARS National, this one is open to all rose growers regardless of residence. Some of the par-ticipants are ARS members who grow hundreds of roses; some are weekend gardeners who have never heard of the organization. However many plants they grow, all competitors pledge that they have raised the roses that they exhibit in their "own private out-door garden."

While shows are open to all, some of the entry classes are re-stricted. National challenge class trophies, such as the Nicholson, are restricted to current ARS members. Challenge class trophies sponsored by an ARS district — in San Diego it was the Pacific

Southwest District — are restricted to members of that district rose society. All other classes, including the class from which Queen of Show will be chosen, are open to all exhibitors regardless of ARS membership or place of residency.

Exhibitors may enter each of the seventy-four horticultural classes as often as they wish, but they may not enter the same variety twice in a class. In other words, Jeff would not be allowed to enter 'Crystalline' twice in class 43 — One Hybrid Tea or Grandiflora Bloom, but he could enter a 'Crystalline' and a 'Lanvin'. In reality, most exhibitors do not waste two great blossoms in one class; instead, they enter their best hybrid tea in the class from which Queen will be chosen, and their second best in the challenge class that they most want to win.

"RACHEL!" On the other side of the room, Cal Hayes hugs Rachel Hunter. She is dressed in a hibiscus-print Hawaiian shirt, canary yellow capri pants, and red slides. Behind her, wheeling a plastic crate of hybrid teas, Phil is in khakis and T-shirt.

"One box?" Cal asks.

"Oh, Cal. Don't even ask!" Rachel's large eyes widen in her freckled, tanned face. "Eighteen hybrid teas. That's it. But I'm still going to try. I'm going to win that Nicholson Trophy, Cal!"

He smiles. "You bet you are. Just not this year."

I cross the room to say hello and narrowly avoid a woman walking blind behind a huge armload of antique rose sprays. Rachel greets me with a hug.

"What time is it? Oh God, 5 a.m. That's all right. No point in getting here early with so few flowers."

Rachel had been right to worry about the heat and wind. Her eighteen blossoms are what remain from an initial harvest of fifty-six that she began cutting and refrigerating fifteen days ago. She cut the last rose seven days ago, just before the weather made further culling pointless. But would any of them survive that length of time in the fridge? Rachel says that she had begun at midnight to rehydrate all fifty-six cuttings by placing the stems in hot water one at a time. By 3 a.m., she figured that eighteen of the flowers looked good enough to show. She woke Phil for a second opinion. He agreed with her assessment. So they showered, packed the roses, and got on the road. Rachel was sleepless, Phil moderately sleepless, but they had eaten their preferred preshow breakfast on the drive from Temecula — chocolate muffins from Costco.

The eighteen candidates look as full and as vibrant as Rachel herself.

"Oh, I don't know!" she trills to herself as she settles on a metal folding chair and positions a rose in its vase on the floor in front of her. She flips open a lilac-colored makeup case. "Zippity-do-dah. I love this thing. It's small, but it holds everything." Inside are tidy trays of Q-tips, rubber bands, white and blue cotton balls. I see tweezers, a magnifying glass, labels, pens, pruners, knife, paint pad to polish leaves, small makeup brush for working centers, needle-nose pliers, serrated scissors, rose show handbook. Guarding the blossom with her hand, Rachel leans forward and whispers loudly, "You know, macho guys don't carry these makeup cases around. They use toolboxes big enough to build a house with. I'm like, 'Come on, guys, get off it!'" She giggles, glances down at the flower, and as suddenly as a flicked switch, the smile vanishes. Elbows steady on her knees, she bends over the flower and begins delicately to adjust petals with her fingers. "Roses rarely are perfect from the bush, so you have to help them out." As she works, her flawless French manicure glints in the bright overhead light.

It's 5:30 a.m. All of the long tables are filled and the room is beginning to smell like a florist's shop. As I head toward the coffee urn, I skirt the big round tables at the back of the room. These tables are farthest from the parking lot entrance, but they, too, are filling fast, mostly with the uninitiated. I spot several people who stand mesmerized in the midst of the action, their one bucket of roses and one pair of shears untouched. A young man with a scruffy beard lays a shrub rose branch that must be four-feet long across a table and asks no one in particular, "Now what?" A fresh-faced man in his thirties pushes past with a two-seater baby carriage. One seat is taken by a sleeping toddler, the other by a bucket of miniature roses. He carries a sleeping infant in a pack on his back. I watch as the man finds a space at the last open table in the corner, retrieves a handful of narrow vases from the registration table and begins to set up. Then, "Oh, excuse me!"

I step back to avoid a slightly stooped woman who is whipping sprays of multicolored floribundas from a vase on one table to a vase on another. She has a concentrated, despairing expression on her face.

"No good, no good, no good," she mumbles. Suddenly, she pulls a pair of needle-nose shears from her shirt pocket and snips off a blossom at the center of a spray. A ruffle of pink falls to the floor. A microsecond of consideration, then snip, another pink decapitation.

A young blond woman stoops to collect the blossoms. "Why did you snip that?"

"Ruined the integrity." She shakes her head and shifts to another spray, "Look at this. It's supposed to be 'City of San Francisco'."

Bob Martin materializes behind her. "Too bad, Lynn."

This must be Lynn Snetsinger of Arcadia, California, who habitually wins National Challenge prizes for the best floribunda and polyantha sprays. She is also the rosarian who gave five cymbidium orchids to Peter Alonso who passed them to Jeff Stage.

"I had to put it in the fridge! It would have blown out if I hadn't picked it and refrigerated it on Friday."

"Quite right." The spring rose season in Bob's Arizona home is already finished, so he's not here to exhibit. Instead, he plans to help his friends and then give an afternoon seminar, "Staging Techniques for Challenge Classes."

"It's supposed to be ruby," mourns Lynn. The rose is deep lilac.

"Mmm. Can't take refrigeration."

"What's the point? They're not worth it. Worst roses I've grown in years. What's the point?"

Bob rests his hand on her shoulder. "Now, Lynn."

Suddenly, she darts out from under Bob's consoling hand to stand in front of two sprays of pale peach floribunda.

"Now these are both fabulous! Not fabulous as my best ever, but fabulous. Maybe, if I . . ." Her sentence trails off as she grasps the sprays. The blonde woman hands her a vase, then turns to me.

"Hi. I'm Suzanne Horn. You here to learn, too?"

I nod.

"I've won some awards locally with my miniatures, but this is my first National." She crosses her arms and shivers with excitement — or cold, I'm not sure. "I'm Lynn's acolyte today. I'm going to pick up every bit of information I can."

Bob nods approvingly and melts away to another table. A

young man with pomaded hair picks up a pair of deckle-edged shears and says in Lynn's direction, "Oh God, it's six o'clock." Lynn reaches for a hot pink spray and pays no attention.

I back away into cardboard boxes that overflow with dried seedpods, baby's breath, spirals of Harry Lauder's Walking Stick, picture frames, decorative bowls, and great chunks of Oasis floral foam. They surround a large woman in a pink rose-patterned dress. She is oblivious to the near disaster, intent instead on inserting a tiny green frond into a teacup filled with miniature roses. An arranger. In fact, I've backed into a bouquet of arrangers, almost all women, who have filled the space between four neighboring tables with provisions for their craft.

Behind me, there is an unmistakable chuckle, and sure enough, I turn to find Clarence standing beside the coffee urn with a steaming paper cup in one hand and an almond cruller in the other.

"Didn't I tell you that you would have a good time?" He beams at me beneath the bill of a purple and green baseball cap, on which BOWERS OF FLOWERS, ARS NATIONAL CONVENTION, SAN DIEGO, MAY 2004 is stitched in pink thread.

"Oh, Clarence! I am so glad to see you."

"Me too," he says. "Have a doughnut. You'll need your strength."

"Did you bring roses?"

"No, no. I just came to watch the grooming and to see who is showing what." A pink-faced fellow calls out, "Clarence! You're here!" Clarence lifts the last bite of cruller in greeting. "No better way to see the newest varieties than come to a show." His grin slips into a serious expression. "Aren't these roses as amazing as I told you they would be?"

I tell him that they are, but there are so many of them that I'm overwhelmed.

"Don't worry." He hands me the doughnut that I had been resisting, chooses one with chocolate sprinkles for himself, and surveys the room. "Now, let's see," he says. "Not too tense yet." He starts to grin again. "But Tommy will be. Let's go see Tommy Cairns."

Our progress is slow because Clarence pauses to greet most of the competitors. We stop beside a small slender woman bent low over a pink and white hybrid tea. Like Rachel, she has set it in a vase on the floor so that she can see into the blossom rather than look at the side of it. She wedges a dark blue cotton pompom between two petals, then stands up to greet us.

Susan Chan McCarthy smiles first with her eyes. Her grave, attractive face is decorated with rimless glasses and framed by long gray-black hair pulled into a loose ponytail. She wears a white sweater, faded blue jeans, white cotton socks, leather Teva sandals. She carries a pair of pruners in a worn leather holster on her belt.

Susan learned her love of gardening from her mother and, in turn, gave her mother a love of roses. First, Lora Lee Chan, a young widow with three children, maintained a San Francisco garden planted with gladiola, dahlias, and seventeen different varieties of fuchsia. When Susan went away to law school her mother moved to a house in San Francisco's Sunset District, a region renowned for salt air and morning fog. Despite the conditions, Susan remembers that her mother raised vegetables, fruit trees, exotic Chinese magnolias, some roses, and many orchids.

"Not just the cybidiums that thrive for everyone in San Francisco, but cattleyas, miltonia, dendrobium, and phalaenopsis," says Susan. "All without a greenhouse."

In 1980, when Susan and her baseball-loving husband, Mike, moved into their first house near San Francisco, they bought a package of three roses from Jackson & Perkins: 'Love', a red grandiflora; 'Honor', a white hybrid tea; and 'Cherish', an orange-pink floribunda.

"Mom would come over to our house to take care of my young children, so it was not long before she had cuttings of these roses growing in her garden."

When Susan, Mike, and the children moved twenty miles south to Hillsborough, Lora Lee made cuttings of her 'Love', 'Honor', and 'Cherish' for their new garden. Susan grows them still in a garden overflowing in hybrid teas, miniatures, and old-garden roses. She believes that she has over two hundred plants, but, she says, "It's hard to get an exact count."

Those two-hundred-odd plants may offer a wealth of blossoms, but they are not helping her right now. "I flew from San Francisco last night, and I didn't pack them right this time. Most of my blossoms were crushed." She adds, "This is 'Lynn Anderson'. Won Queen with her at the 2002 Spring National. This one is still so young that her petals don't want to pull apart at all. But she has a center, not crushed, you see?" As we start to look, she adds, "Evidently she's a singer."

We peer down at the top of the rose named for a country music star whose album *Rose Garden* went platinum in 1970. It does have a perfect central tip opening into a symmetrical, overlapping spiral of pristine petals. But ARS show rules dictate that the blossom of a perfect Queen must be one-half to three-quarters open. This rose isn't more than one-quarter open. Susan inserts two more Q-tips near the top of the bloom, pulls a strand of powder blue cotton fluff from a small cardboard box, and gently packs the fluff between several of the lower petals, forcing them apart. She stands up and sighs.

"She just needs to relax," she says, and before I can ask, adds, "I use the blue cotton fluff because it's more visible than white. People have been known to leave the white fluff in by mistake during a show. When the judging starts, it's too late to remove it."

I start to ask if she's ever done such a thing, but she interrupts me with a Mona Lisa smile and lifts down a deep pink hybrid tea with smoky edges. I inhale the blossom's clove fragrance but keep my nose well away from the petals. Damaging a competitor's blossom guarantees excommunication from the rose world.

"Nice scent," Susan agrees. "Not that it matters."

Like Kitty Belendez, Susan loves the scent of her favorite flower. She relishes hybrid teas such as 'Dolly Parton', which boasts huge, strongly scented orange-pink blossoms. The blooms are so large, says Susan, that "some rosarians compare them to Dolly Parton's — mmm, her endowment — though it's mostly men who make that comparison." She has kept the show-stopping yellow-pink floribunda 'Sheila's Perfume', even though she does "not crave" floribunda trophies. "If I were strong, I would take her out." Susan shakes her head and picks up a pompom. "But I love her, so I keep her." The bemused tone of voice makes it clear that she sees herself as a pushover. Holding the pompom between fore and middle fingers, she slides it between two petals. Suddenly, a rose that had looked good now looks perfect or, at least, perfectly symmetrical.

" 'Barbra Streisand'." Susan shakes her head. "I know that petal will bounce back when I take the ball out. She's temperamental, just like her namesake."

Her comment reminds me of Eleanor Roosevelt, who was also

honored with a rose in her name: "I was very flattered. But I was not pleased to read the description in the catalogue: 'no good in a bed, but fine up against a wall.'"

"Holy shit! That thing had an affair with an avocado!" Rachel has appeared at the table beside Susan's. Geri Minot McCarron, who is tidying rose foliage lets her deckle-edged scissors drop with a clatter and bursts out laughing. She and Rachel have each kept the promise to enter this National. Once she arrived, though, she had picked a table across the room from Rachel believing that she might be able to concentrate better away from her best friend. No dice.

"You're not trying to trim that thing, are you, Geri?" Geri nods, helpless, as Rachel picks up the rose in its vase and shows it about. "I mean look at this!"

Beside me, Susan, says, "She's right. Those leaves must be six inches long."

"Look at the bloom, Rachel," pleads Geri. Rachel examines the pristine, pale 'Marilyn Monroe' and nods.

"Exquisite," she says. "But the leaves, Geri. They're gigantic."

"Maybe so," Geri concedes. "But you know I won Queen with 'Marilyn Monroe' at the California Coastal Rose Society show last week — my first Queen." She gives a shiver of nervous excitement. "If the leaves really are too big on this one, I have others. But this bloom . . ." Her sentence trails off as she returns to the rose.

"I wish I had others." Rachel groans with mock-real pain and abandons Geri to her pinking shears.

Geri cuts slivers from the massive leaves. "When the winds picked up again last week, I almost gave up. Then I remembered our promise. I've worked a hundred hours on my roses this week."

She stops cutting. Unconsciously, she holds the shears aloft like a sword pointing the way into battle. "This week ..."

Her husband, Alan, lifts his head of blond curls at the far end of the table where he has been filling out tags. "This week we're looking for crystal."

At the neighboring table, Susan continues to groom, a pool of quiet in the room's controlled storm of activity.

"Are you indicating that you want me to go away, Tommy?"

Clarence and I turn to see Steve Jones addressing Tommy Cairns, who is either oblivious or pointedly not listening.

I had heard that Tommy and Steve once had a shouting match at a local show when Tommy was showing and Steve was judging. I had also been told that their relationship had marginally improved. Being a rose show judge is not like being a judge at the Olympics, where the men and women who hold up numbered placards are not active athletes. In a rose show, today's exhibitor may be tomorrow's judge and vice versa, so it is wise to control one's temper.

Tommy says that he has mellowed since his 2002 heart bypass surgery. He concentrates on the awards he really wants rather than becoming frenzied about them all.

"I even walk around the prep room, now, to greet my fellow competitors. I never would have done that in previous years."

Perhaps I did see his slender form moving whippetlike through the room earlier, but *mellow* is not the operative word. Tommy whirls back and forth between two rose-covered tables. He reaches, positions, snips, whips one spray out of a vase, puts another spray in, stands back with his arms crossed, frowns, removes the rose, begins again.

Luis Desamero, in Polo shirt, blue shorts, and a baseball cap, sits at a third table that is thicketed with miniature roses in every conceivable color. Luis reaches out, selects a bloom, turns it this way and that, and more often than not, sets it back in the green plastic florist supply container from whence it came. No Albertson's milk or Tropicana orange juice containers here. After close examination, he puts a yellow 'Luis Desamero' in a four-inch-diameter bowl.

"For the Luis Desamero." He glances up beneath the bill of his cap. Luis and Tommy sponsor an ARS Pacific Southwest District trophy named the Luis Desamero Challenge Bowl. It demands eighteen miniature roses, one bloom per stem, six or more varieties, displayed in a bowl no wider than four inches. Evidently, Luis plans to win it himself this year with at least one 'Luis Desamero' in the bowl.

Next he trims the stem of a pink blossom to three inches and slips the shortened flower into a hole in a flat-topped, eight-inch-square wooden container called an English box. Only the blooms are visible in an English box, like decapitated rose heads. Snip, he cuts off a ruby rose and slides it into an eight-hole English box. He tilts his head, birdlike, considers, then lifts the rose and slides it into the neighboring hole.

"Here, Steve, a rose." This is why Steve has come to this whirlwind section of the room. Luis selects a pretty pink mini from a vase and cuts its stem to a lapel-perfect three inches. He offers it to Steve, who puts it in his buttonhole.

It is 7:45 a.m. The noise in the room now sounds like a hive of angry bees. I've got to check on Jeff Stage. As I turn, a wild-eyed, Hawaiian-shirted man runs by me carrying a sloshing bucket of water. Another young man with a mop of uncombed ginger hair stands in the center aisle between tables holding a bunch of entry tags. I hear him ask the air, "What if I don't remember the name of my rose? What do I write?" His hands shake.

I am diverted by the sight of Satish and Vijaya Prabhu, who have arrived late to a corner of the table next to Cal Hayes. They work intently and move around each other as if in a dance. She kneels before an array of mini-floras, wipes foliage, and rises effortlessly. He bends over a row of nine hybrid teas, shifts a pink blossom from one end to the other. He moves the vases to form a V, then an upside-down V. He removes a bloom that is shaded with the faintest hint of orange, then catches me watching and smiles. "The only thing more frustrating than making an orange rose fit is playing golf."

Satish and Vijaya flew in last night. Satish had been right to be worried. Early May is simply too early for most roses in his garden. If he had not been scheduled to give a 1 p.m. lecture, "Staging Hybrid Tea Challenge Classes," they might not have come at all. Now, though, he is staying in fighting trim by working with the small number of mini-floras and hybrid teas that they did bring. He is staging the Nicholson, which he last won in 1989 after driving nonstop from Columbia to Kansas City with Vijaya and their two daughters. Might this year be his second chance?

"Oh my, there is always a chance." He lifts a finger as a teacher does to quiet a class. "But it is up to the roses and the judges — and my stamina."

There was a time when he would have groomed his blooms all night. In 1986 in Oklahoma City, he advanced, or opened, the petals of a 'Color Magic' with cotton balls throughout the night.

"I advanced one petal every half hour; any faster and the petals would have bounced back or broken. Every now and again, Vijaya would wake up and say, 'What are you doing?'

"'I'm advancing the rose.'

"'You're crazy; go to bed!'

"'I'll be right there,' I'd say, and keep on working. You have to be very patient to do that, but I had to do it, because even though that rose was too tight, I didn't have another one of that quality."

The rose gave Satish his only National Queen.

"Satish?" Vijaya gestures toward ten mini-floras with pristine foliage that she has organized in vases at the end of the table.

"I'll let you both get back to work," I say. She rewards me with a beautiful smile.

I turn toward Cal. Fourteen Q-tipped roses are marshaled before him. Like the Prabhus and Susan Chan McCarthy, he is a study in calm compared to the swirl of activity at other tables.

"Getting down to decision time," he greets me. "Only nine of these girls are going to the party." He adjusts a Q-tip, considers, moves another. Dampens a finger and rubs it over a leaf. The roses range from carmine red to hot pink to a pale pink–tinged white. Abruptly, he moves the carmine hybrid tea to the middle of the row and begins to move the other blooms to form a horse-shoe shape with the carmine rose at the top.

"Won this five times and always used this presentation." He removes a rose from the table. "I want to win it one more time; then I'm on the road out. Of course, I said that when I wanted to win it for the third time."

He lifts the center rose from its vase, trims a quarter inch from the bottom of the stem and sets it back in the water. "Last thing my wife said to me as I went out the door was, 'Remember, judges don't like 'em high,'" he explains.

Cal and Barb Hayes have been married since 1951. This is the first time since 1987 that he has attended a show without her. Instead of helping him groom, Barb is watching their granddaughter compete in an NCAA water polo match.

He moves two hot pink hybrid teas to the fourth position on each side of the horseshoe.

"I was a manufacturing manager before I retired. Barb says that roses have been the best thing in the world for me. Come home from work and get out into the yard to relieve tension. But I'm seventy-four years old. Getting too old to take care of the roses."

"How many do you have?"

"Oh, I don't know really. Maybe four hundred." He pulls four Q-tips — pluck, pluck pluck, pluck — from three roses. Another blossom is removed from the presentation.

"This is the only hobby I have. If I didn't have roses to get me into the yard, I'd go crazy." Another Q-tip is plucked. "Even in card games I love to win. You're not sitting at the card table just for the company. No sir."

Jeff has switched to the other side of his table so that he can't see Cal.

"Hello, hello, hello. Come to watch me cry?" I notice slender trickles of sweat on Jeff's forehead.

"That bad?"

"These roses are coming up to perfection and going right past. Why stop for judgment hour at 9:30, when you can break Jeff's heart at 8 a.m.?" He stands with arms akimbo behind a burgundy hybrid tea, Q-tip in his right hand.

"I've given up on going for the Nicholson Trophy. Not enough varieties that look good. But the Herb Swim Trophy is mine, definitely mine. See these?" He points to six different varieties of hybrid tea — deep ruby to the palest cream. "Just need five of them to be perfect. This one's a possible." He adds a Q-tip. "If one Q-tip is good, three are better. I've gone as high as twenty Q-tips."

I decide not to mention that Cal Hayes has reached the Q-tip removal stage.

Jeff grasps an offending petal between thumb and forefinger and rocks it gently back and forth until the petal releases. Then he shifts the two neighboring petals so that the lower one rests on top. He stands back: a big, bristly man in front of a slender, thorny rose.

"So?"

So a rose that had looked fine to my eyes looks finer; it's more circular and less cluttered.

"Pretty," I say.

"Pretty? Did you say pretty?" He yells dramatically, his eyes wide open, his eyebrows pumping up and down. Kitty Belendez looks up from a froth of peach floribunda that she is trimming with toenail clippers.

"Jeff, be nice."

"Whew!" He stops just as dramatically and wipes a hand across his brow. "Never call a competitor's roses 'pretty.' 'Gorgeous,' perhaps, or 'fantastic.' 'Pretty' is for girls."

"Hey, break a stem, Stage." Kitty rises from her bent pruning position and brandishes her nail clippers.

AT THAT MOMENT, huge accordion doors at the edge of the room clunk open. On the other side is yet another bright white ballroom, this one filled with long rows of tables draped in ivory cloth. The center of the room is dominated by a big, square, three-tiered, white-covered table — the trophy table — encrusted with crystal vases and silver urns, bowls, and platters. In the doorway, standing behind a long table, are ten men and women wearing orange vests.

"Ho, ho! The race is on," says Jeff. It is eight thirty.

At the neighboring table, Ron Gregory gives a small startled jump as the door opens. His roses are set in a horseshoe shape that matches Cal's.

Jeff calls across, "Don't worry, Ron. Your roses are looking better than Cal's. Everyone says so." As he turns back to a ruby hybrid tea, he tells me that he has critiqued both men's entries and believes that Ron's really is slightly better than Cal's.

Five tables away, Cal looks up and smiles. He gives a small nod, then moves one more rose off to the side. Only nine blooms remain on his table.

Luis zips by carrying an English box in each hand. He sets them on the long table where two of the men wearing orange vests pick them up and carry them into the exhibition hall. Competitors in the challenge classes like the Nicholson are allowed to set their own roses in the hall because staging — how the vases are positioned — is part of the score. Submissions for all other categories, including class 43 — One Hybrid Tea or Grandiflora Bloom from which the judges will choose Queen, must be put on the table for runners to take in.

On the other side of Cal, Rachel's roses are luscious and full. Too full? She shakes her head and bites her lip.

"I've stopped working them. They're going past." She gives a little laugh. "We need to have the judging right this very second."

"Well then, let's at least take them in." Phil reaches for the pale pink hybrid tea nearest him. Rachel sits back down.

"You take that one. I'm just going to make a slight adjustment . . . " Her sentence trails off as she sets a dark pink blossom on the floor in front of her.

I follow Phil into the exhibition hall. Orange-vested men and women dart about the white room holding vases and boxes of roses. Here and there, an exhibitor or arranger crouches over an entry. I recognize Peter Alonso on the far side of the room. He stands in front of a clear bowl that spills over in a rainbow of miniature blossoms; he turns the bowl minutely, examines the effect, turns it again. A cardboard placard near the bowl reads A-8. I leaf quickly through my program. Class 8 is the Dee Bennett Memorial Trophy — twelve miniature roses in a clear container.

Phil heads toward a long table in the near left corner of the room marked A-1 for the Nicholson Perpetual Challenge Bowl. He sets the pale pink rose near the end of the table and retreats.

Voices rise in the corner behind the Nicholson section. A man and a woman lean over an arrangement of three black frames and a rose. She gestures and it's clear that they differ — politely, tensely — about the angle of the third frame. It's Cynthia Chuang and her husband, Chi Ning Liu, the man who has sacrificed his status in the family to roses. Their disagreement ends with a minute shift of the frame and many nods and smiles. I follow Phil out the door just as a frowning runner advances toward me. Without an exhibitor to assist, I have no right to be in the room.

Within minutes, the runner appears beside Rachel holding the pink rose that Phil had just taken into the exhibition hall.

"Thought you'd want to fix this."

Rachel lifts her head. Phil groans and clips off the small white tag that they had used to identify the rose in the storage cooler.

"Thank you, thank you."

"Sure." Rose in hand, the man trots off.

Phil picks up two more roses and follows him. Rachel looks down at the hybrid tea she's grooming and sighs.

"I've got to pull this petal out. Hate like hell to do it, but I have to." She sounds like a surgeon saying, "That leg must go."

Across the room, Kitty slides five vases of floribunda to the end of her table. "Okay, this is it. I've made my selection. Bob?" She whirls around looking for her husband, who raises his head above the garden of flowers at the far end of the table.

"The tags —"

"I'm already working on them." He arrives beside her with a packet of long, tan cardboard tags in his hand.

"These are for the floribunda sprays." Kitty points to two vibrant bunches of crimson. Bob writes " 'Sexy Rexy' " and " 'Lavaglut' " on the top section of two tags, folds them so that the "Bob and Kitty Belendez" notation at the bottom of the tags doesn't show, attaches the tags to the vases, and carries them over to the long table.

As he works, Kitty shifts from foot to foot. "Oh my, oh my. I was sure we could do the Pacific Challenge —" This demands five different floribunda sprays. "But Bob, what are the Buck rules again?"

Bob reads aloud the entrance requirement for the Dr. Griffith Buck National Memorial Trophy: "*Three different shrub varieties, one bloom or spray (two or more blooms), exhibited in three separate containers.*"

"Okay, fine." She holds up two vases of floribunda. Her head looks from one to the other as if watching a tennis match. Finally,

"This one is brighter." It holds 'Abraham Darby', 'Perdita', and 'William Shakespeare 2000'. This last has a wonderful purplish red blossom with a multiplicity of petals.

"You've got to cut that bud off. It's your weak point." Andrew Platz, the man who had greeted Clarence hours before, had stopped beside Clarence and me to watch Kitty compare the two vases of floribunda.

"Okay." Kitty nods. "Tools!" she calls. Bob hands her a pair of needle-nose snips. As Clarence, Andrew, Bob, and I stand around her like attentive acolytes, she severs the offending bud as close as possible to the main stem.

"Yes!" She has left no scar, although she does push one small blossom over another to improve the symmetry. Bob starts to fill out the tags.

Andrew trails off toward Cal's table. He reappears soon, holding one of Cal's hybrid teas before him as an alter boy holds a candle.

"Ha! Cal's on the move," says Clarence.

Cal Hayes says, "Hi there," as he passes. Ron Gregory blanches and looks at his own blooms. Decisively, he exchanges one vased rose for another, then nods.

"Here, Ron," says Jeff. "Ready to go?"

"As I'll ever be."

Jeff Stage sets down the tag that he has been filling out for his Herb Swim entry and picks up a vase. Ron picks up two. Other men appear to collect the last of the entry. Not quite the formal procession that accompanied Cal, but it is only Ron's first try for the award.

At the drop-off table, Susan Chan McCarthy sets down the

'Lynn Anderson'. She offers a wry smile and shakes her head. "She's too young, can't seem to hold her petals open."

Up walks the man with two children. The baby on his back is still, or perhaps again, asleep six hours later. The child in the stroller is wide awake and walking. Tongue caught between her teeth, she carefully sets a small vase containing a miniature rose on the table.

"Good job." Her father is carrying six vases of minis in a precarious two-fisted grip.

The table fills with roses. The runners pick up, read the tag, trot away, and return empty handed; pick up, read the tag, . . . "Hey!" A runner calls after the pomaded young man who had earlier been hanging around Lynn Snetsinger. He holds up a fully open hybrid tea. "No tag! Did you leave this?"

The young man scurries back. He must have left the tag on the prep table.

"Next time I won't call you. No tag — immediate disqualification."

"Yes, yes. Oh God, I'm sorry." He races off with the rose.

I peer around the corner into the hall. Cal stands in front of his Nicholson entry with a clump of men standing close behind him. He leans in, shifts a vase slightly to the right. Heads nod. Edges another vase to the left. The men behind him confer. He pays no attention.

"Got to get Ron a group of followers," says Jeff as he walks swiftly by with two hybrid teas.

Beside Cal, Rachel and Phil arrange eight of her roses in two straight lines perpendicular to the table edge — dark at the back, lightest in front. The ninth rose is set equidistant between the lines, crowning the presentation.

On the other side of the table, Satish Prabhu stages his Nicholson in an upside-down V. Across the room, I see Vijaya working with a cluster of mini-floras. She stands back, moves one vase, stands back, moves another. Satish walks away from his Nicholson, turns and scouts along the table, looking at his presentation in profile.

The Hayes, Prabhus, Hunters, and Ron Gregory are the only exhibitors competing for the Nicholson this year. Bob Martin has told me that this Spring National is a small show compared with earlier years. The heat wave in southern California decimated most local exhibitors' roses, not just Rachel's. And for the rest of the country, this show was either too early or too far away. The result has been fewer exhibitors with fewer blooms. The exhibition hall may look like a huge rose garden to me, but it should look like the mother of all rose gardens.

At the far end of the prep room, Tommy Cairns dashes from one table to another, carrying vases of roses. The heat wave didn't affect his garden. Click! He sets the vases down in front of Andrew, who has moved from advising Kitty and carrying Cal's roses to assisting Tommy. " 'Mercedes' and 'Honey Perfume'." He races back to the prep table, returns with two more. " 'Lavaglut' and 'Playgirl'."

Andrew scribbles. He is helping fill out Tommy's tags.

" 'Passionate Kisses'. Got it? Good. We're off." They race-walk through the room with vases of flowers. In the show room, they hesitate, scanning tables for section A-6. Ah, over there, beneath a chandelier. Gently, gently, they place the vases and race-walk back to five old-garden roses waiting on the prep table.

"For the Joseph J. Kern Trophy," says Tommy. *Five varieties of old garden rose, properly labeled and displayed in separate containers.* He grabs a handful of tags, hands some to Andrew, begins to scribble. Soon he looks up.

"Yes?" Andrew is writing as fast as he can. It is 9:28 a.m.

"Yes," he says.

They seize the vases and almost run.

10

Judgment Hour

 "So," says a man beside me.

"What a mess," says another as he surveys the strew of tipped vases, puddles, rose bits and blossoms, Q-tips, and squashed cotton balls.

After the huge accordion doors clank shut, the prep room roar dissolves into groans, tired conversation, threads of laughter. Exhibitors throw refuse into oversized gray trash bins and empty vases into buckets, buckets into the sink. They wipe down tables; click shut their toolboxes; try to palm off their remaining flowers.

This is the most difficult time, says Tommy Cairns — "the time when you must turn your back and act nonchalant for the next four hours."

Behind the giant doors, judging teams heft the thick ARS handbook *Guidelines for Judging Roses* and fan out among the tables. The book describes everything from how each entry should be judged to who may become a judge. It is required reading for exhibitors, as well as show organizers and judges, for it details the rose-scoring system.

Satish Prabhu says that while he grew beautiful roses, he did not win blue ribbons at his first shows because he did not know what the judges were looking for. After he bought a copy of the guidelines, he learned that an "exhibition form" hybrid tea is one-half to three-quarters open, perfectly shaped with many symmetrically arranged petals that spiral toward a high center.

"Once we found that guidance, it was easy," explains Vijaya. "The very next spring, we exhibited at the Columbia, South Carolina, rose show and we won everything except Queen."

Satish takes up the tale. "Then we went to Charlotte, North Carolina, and won everything — A to Z. Queen, King, all the Court, every challenge class — the entire table of big roses was ours. That was our second year of showing. Growing roses was not a problem. We just had to learn what they were expecting."

Would that most exhibitors could win every award at a local show the second year out. Yet Satish's point is important: for rose shows to work, exhibitors and judges must use the same criteria.

A rose is judged on the basis of six weighted criteria. In *Showing Good Roses,* Bob Martin writes that while it is important to know the relative value of each criterion, "do not imagine for a moment that the judges actually try to point-score every rose. In fact they rarely do so at all because if they did it would take all day and the winner would be the last rose to fade." Nonetheless, the scores assigned to each criterion "make a valuable point of reference for communication and decision making."

So rose blossom "form" is worth 25 points of the 100-point ARS scoring system.

Color is worth 20 points. By color, the guidelines mean the degree to which a rose's named color matches an idealized version; in other words, how true a salmon color is this salmon-colored rose?

Substance, which is worth 15 points, refers to the texture of the petals — their newness, crispness, thickness.

A long, straight stem and clean, symmetrical foliage are awarded 20 points. Think of the exhibitors who trashed roses with curved stems and who spent hours buffing, polishing, and trimming foliage. All for 20 relative points.

Balance and proportion receive 10 points. Bob Martin says this is one of those "you-know-it-when-you-see-it kind of tests."

"In theory," writes Bob, "the stem must be long enough to complement the size of the bloom; but it should not be too long nor too short. Also, the foliage must be sufficient to frame the bloom but must not be too large or undersized in relation to the bloom."

Balance and proportion may be worth only 10 points, but they are a source of contention between rose societies. The differences between each region's preferred show rose — large blooms on long stems versus smaller blooms on shorter stems — have led to "stem wars" when exhibitors from different locales come together at national shows.

They have also led to stem wars in local societies where exhibitors try to gain a judge's first glance by exhibiting longer-stemmed roses than their competitors. Suzy Bridges, who runs Bridges Roses, a miniature-rose nursery with her husband, Dennis, says, "People have come to the conclusion that for challenge classes and Queen of Show possibilities, you can win without being the best if you catch the judge's eye first. Most judges approach and scan, particularly at a table of ten entries. Sometimes judges will forget to scrutinize the rose they see first."

Suzy believes that stem length should be limited. "It makes a nice uniform display and the public sees the roses so much better if they are all the same height," she explains. One Winston-Salem rose society actually slides competition roses through a rectangular frame; if the rose in its vase does not fit underneath, it doesn't enter the show. "Now, I like that," says Suzy, "but most exhibitors wouldn't."

Size of bloom is awarded 10 points. Again, a judge is asked to compare the rose being judged to an ideal and to award more points for one that exceeds the average. And again, bloom size can be a source of contention between exhibitors — and judges — in different parts of the country.

Judges may not compete in shows they judge. It's a sensible regulation that nevertheless irks some exhibitors, including Bob Martin, who for years resisted becoming a judge. To become accredited, an apprentice judge must work five shows over three years. Bob couldn't decide which shows to judge instead of exhibit. The conundrum stymied him until 1995 when he moved to a new house with a garden full of young, not-yet-competitive plants. He used the enforced break to become a judge.

"Judging is a wonderful experience. It is 'prioritizing beauty,'" he quotes Dr. John Dickman, a retired biochemist from Ohio whose passion for rose-growing and judging is rivaled by his devotion to collecting rose-patterned stamps from around the world.

Bob, who is known to effuse about the loveliness of a table of blooms before pronouncing judgment, says that he has become a much better exhibitor since training to be a judge. Susan Chan McCarthy also says that judging others' exhibits causes her to examine her own entries with a dispassionate eye.

"I'm tougher on my own entries than the nonjudge exhibitor, because when you have judged for a while, you know why something is a better entry than something else."

For Susan, judges are like teachers. When she judged arrangements at a small show in Monterey, California, years ago, there
was only one entry.

"Obviously a beginner because the arrangement was already
losing substance and drooping all over. I bent over backward and
gave it a blue ribbon; then I talked to the arranger about how to
fix it."

Susan asked the host society to allow the arranger to disas-
semble her creation, recut the stems under warm water to stop
the droop, and rearrange it under Susan's direction. "She learned
something and that's what you strive to do at a local show."

A show's chair of judges assigns the judges, who work in
teams. They are assisted by volunteer clerks who attach ribbons
to judged entries. In San Diego six three-judge teams, each assisted by two clerks, critiqued arrangements. Fifteen three-judge
teams, also assisted by two clerks each, critiqued the horticulture entries.

Judges work fast and thoroughly, seeing qualities in the blooms
that are apparent only to skilled eyes. Among the vital esoterica
they memorized at judging school are the characteristics of at
least one hundred different varieties of roses in the hybrid tea,
grandiflora, floribunda, miniature, climber, and antique classes.
Thus, judges must know how many petals are typical of the antique 'Souvenir de la Malmaison', how much variation occurs in
the bicoloration of hybrid tea 'Gemini', and what size leaves are
usual on the miniature 'Kristin'.

In the simpler horticulture classes, their conversations often
sound something like this:

"Second" (spoken in unison). Next rose.

"First." Next rose.

"Also first, don't you think?"

"Yes." The judges continue down the line, speaking quickly. One clerk wields a hole punch over the entry tag. A second clerk pulls a red, white, or blue ribbon from a three-pocket apron and attaches it to the vase. Sounds simple, but having clerked at a local rose show, I can attest that the experience can be a fumbling blur.

"That color is all wrong." The judges frown at a bluish red rose.

"It should be scarlet." They speak together — "Third" — and move down the line.

"Second."

"First."

"Ah, look at that substance."

"Thick, heavy petals. A first, don't you think?"

"Definitely. First."

Judges are not supposed to touch the flowers they evaluate, although it does happen. Suzy Bridges's entry for the Horace McFarland Memorial Award was moved by the judges at a National once.

"I staged the roses in a semicircle because all my blooms tilted a little. That format minimized the tilt. But when it was judged, my McFarland was in a straight line and the blooms touched." Two years later she received a written apology from the show chairman.

Suzy has also had her roses placed in the wrong section by runners, which disqualifies the bloom. This happens at the local and national level more often than anyone wishes. "Last year in Charlotte, I had the prettiest 'Veteran's Honor'. It was just gorgeous.

But placement put it in the wrong section. I didn't notice the problem until judging for Queen had started and the chairman said it was too late to do anything." She laughs and groans simultaneously. "It was a mistake. You just have to let it go, although you really want to scream, 'But it was my best rose!'"

Judges treat entries at the novice table different from those of experienced exhibitors. When I clerked for Sandy Lundberg at a local show, she and partner Doug Craver had halted in front of a dark pink bud on the beginner's table.

"Honorable mention." Doug was ready to move on.

"Perhaps we should make it a third," offered Sandy, her drawl softening the disagreement. The other clerk, with hole punch poised over the Honorable Mention box on the entry tag, stopped just in time. Sandy and Doug peered down at the tiny blossom.

"I know there's some insect damage on the foliage." Sandy pointed to small brown holes on a leaf. "And the stem is not all that straight." She smiled. The stem had a distinct tilt to the right. "But the blossom is fresh and it has good form."

"Not too bad, I guess. Third?"

"Third," they agreed. Judges want to critique honestly, but they don't want to discourage new exhibitors. As Sandy says, "Ribbons can keep you growing roses."

When the judge/clerk teams finish a class, other clerks collect blue-ribbon winners into one section. The judges vote among these winners to select the trophy-winning best in each class — Best Miniature Floating Rose, Best English Box, and so on. Blue-ribbon hybrid teas that are eligible for the Queen and her Court are balloted last in a procedure that I call the Dance of the Queen.

The Dance of the Queen resembles a whooping crane mating dance minus the crane's stick-tossing. Judges circle a table on which all the blue-ribbon hybrid teas are displayed. At many local shows, they pull forward the best of the best and push back the worst of the best. At national shows, candidate roses are chosen from the blue-ribbon pool by ballot.

Once final candidates are selected, serious circling begins. Not allowed to touch, judges bend, squat, lean and tiptoe as they go round and round. The shortest judges jump to see into the blossoms and taller judges crouch low to examine rose profiles. Knees crack as they stand. Judges hold little paper ballots on which they list their five favorites in order; majority rules. First balloting chooses Queen, second balloting Princess, and so on. The entire process is repeated for the Miniature Queen and Court.

Finally, trophy winners are moved to the prize-covered central table and losers are left to wilt where they were staged.

WHILE THEY WAIT, most exhibitors eat breakfast. In San Diego a large group took over half the booths and tables in a Mexican restaurant for huevos rancheros and pancakes. After breakfast, they attend ARS seminars designed to alleviate impatience. At noon Jeff Stage presented to a standing-room-only crowd "Grooming the Bloom." At 12:30 Andrew Platz discussed how to stage old-garden rose challenge classes. By 1:00, the audience was growing tense, so Satish Prabhu offered as much dry wit as information during his talk on staging hybrid tea challenge classes. At 1:25 he said, "I will end now; most of us have a 1:30 deadline."

While exhibitors educated each other, rose show visitors

massed in front of the Grand Ballroom's double doors. Those who had attended their colleagues' seminars now found themselves at the back of the throng. At 1:40, when the doors swung open, so many people surged toward the three-tiered trophy table that most couldn't get near it.

Some never tried. Visitors not interested in Queen of Show scattered through the ballroom to record the names of other enticing blooms. Exhibitors who hoped for a blue ribbon instead of a trophy made a beeline toward their entries. I spotted the man with two children wheeling the baby carriage toward section K, where the novice entries clustered. As he and the children examined the miniatures he'd entered, the toddler began to clap.

The crowd around the trophy table was still five deep when Geri McCarron popped suddenly out of the press of bodies. She wrapped her arms around herself and shivered. Her face was chalk white.

"Queen." Her voice was thin with shock. "My 'Marilyn Monroe' took Queen." The rose with avocado-sized leaves had trumped other entries as Queen of Show and won a Best in Show Trophy sponsored by GardenWeb.

"I'm dumbfounded," she whispered, shaking. "I worked a hundred hours on my roses this week, worked beyond pain the way an athlete does." She stared at her husband, Alan, who grinned so broadly that his face could have split. Abruptly, Geri started to laugh. "We won!" she cried. They dove back into the melee around the table.

"Do not give up, Ron. You will learn from this one. There is always next year." Satish's precise voice was warm with comfort. He and Ron Gregory stood in the crowd before Cal Hayes's perfect winning entry for the Nicholson Perpetual Challenge Bowl. Cal had left hours ago to attend his granddaughter's water polo match. His competitors were left to cope with the news he'd won for a record sixth time.

"I thought I had it." Ron's face drooped. "I exchanged one of the flowers just before staging. Perhaps . . ." He trailed off.

"Perhaps," agreed Satish. "But you have two roses in the Court of Honor."

Ron perked up. His mauve 'Natasha Monet' and deep pink 'Big Time' glowed on the far side of Geri's Queen.

"And *you* won the Ben Williams Mini-Flora Trophy," he replied. The mini-floras on which Vijaya Prabhu had been so intent colored a corner of the trophy table.

A shift of bodies revealed Susan Chan McCarthy pausing in front of her 'Lynn Anderson', which had won Princess of Show. The blossom was so exquisite that I wondered why it hadn't won Queen.

"It's a matter of timing," Susan replied equably as people jostled us for a clear view. "She was too tight when the show was judged; now she's perfect. Whereas 'Marilyn Monroe'" — she gestured toward the Queen, which had opened beyond exhibition stage — "*she* was perfect at the judgment hour." Susan sighed, "There's a lesson about life in this somewhere."

For all their regulated rose care and record keeping, exhibitors compete in a field in which they are not in charge. No matter how well they prepare, they are at the mercy of their blooms. Success or failure often rests on a single petal. Even when they succeed, their prize-winning creation crumples and dies within hours. The Buddhists teach that everything in life is continuously changing. In the exhibiting world, too, nothing lasts forever — not bad weather, a plague of Japanese beetles, not the most exquisite flower.

Tommy Cairns stood still amid the swell. Three prep tables full of flowers and intense deliberation had reaped reward. He and Luis had won six challenge trophies, the most ever by an individual exhibitor or team at a National. Amid the triumph, though, one regret — Tommy had lost the Joseph J. Kern Trophy for old-garden roses to Lillian Biesiadecki, who specializes in antique varieties.

"It was that rush to label my entries just before prep time closed." He grimaced when I asked him. "I made a mistake, misidentified a blossom. It's what I tell others — 'You will slip up if you hurry.' I should have known better."

Oblivious to bodies bumping her, Kitty Belendez bent over a cluster of flowers. "All right, that's better." She repositioned two vases from her winning entry for the Dr. Griffith Buck Memorial Trophy. "Yes, thank you, we're pleased," she said when I congratulated her. Intent on making her winner look as perfect as when she had staged it, she didn't smile. "They got the order wrong when they moved our roses to the trophy table. I don't want anyone wondering why we won."

Despite the crush, the crowd was quiet, almost subdued. Geri McCarron had shivered, but neither she nor any other exhibitor screamed with delight or shock. No one cried or danced a celebratory jig. No one gave an overly long speech thanking their parents, spouses, or God. Instead, they circled and peered and nodded, their faces tight with concentration as they took notes. Already, it seemed, they were planning for the future. The next show, new varieties, new equipment, a better way to persuade the deep pink petals of 'Hot Princess' to open symmetrically.

Awards are important, but as it turns out, they are not the ulti-mate goal. A rose show is more about the process of winning than about the win. It is about meeting the challenge of choosing the right roses and tending them well; transporting, grooming, and staging them as skillfully as you possibly can; and doing it better next time. For many exhibitors, the run for the roses beats cross-ing the finish line.

Jeff Stage had won the Herb Swim Memorial, but Jeff him-self was nowhere in sight. In fact, he had known that he'd won the Swim since 12:30, when a friend who had clerked the show gave him the news. Jeff had also won the Guy Blake Hedrick Jr. Award, which honors the lifetime achievement of a winning ex-hibitor who works unusually hard to encourage and advise other exhibitors. He was thrilled, but by the time the show opened at 1:40 he had wanted to make a quick tour of the trophy table and take a nap. Rachel and Phil Hunter had also gone off to sleep af-ter determining that Rachel had not won the Nicholson, which was the only class she'd entered.

Giving advance notice of a win or loss is officially frowned upon by the ARS, but it happens often — so often that by the time a National opens, half the trophy candidates may already know who won the big awards. Even exhibitors who don't know in advance who won learn to look toward the table where they staged their roses. If their entry is missing, it's on the trophy table. If not, there is always next year.

A Selected List of Winners from the ARS Spring National Rose Show, San Diego, CA

NATIONAL CHALLENGE CLASSES

Nicholson Perpetual Challenge
 Bowl
Cal & Barbara Hayes
'Andrea Stelzer', 'Cajun Moon',
 'Cajun Sunrise', 'Crystalline',
 'Hot Princess', 'Moonstone',
 'Natasha Monet', 'Signature',
 'Veteran's Honor'

C. Eugene Pfister Memorial Trophy
Dr. Thomas Cairns & Luis
 Desamero
'Rejoice'

New Zealand Kiwi Award
Dr. Thomas Cairns & Luis
 Desamero
'Andrea Stelzer', 'Touch of Class',
 'Moonstone', 'Signature',
 'Cotillion', 'Playgirl'

Joseph J. Kern Trophy
Lillian Biesiadecki
'Baronne Prévost', 'Comte de
 Chambord', 'Rose de Rescht',
 'Sombreuil', 'Yolande d'Aragon'

Dorothy C. Stemler Memorial
 Award
Dr. Thomas Cairns & Luis
 Desamero
'Baronne Prévost', 'Comtesse de
 Murinais', 'Marchesa Boccella',
 'Reine Victoria', 'Salet',
 R. rugosa alba

William H. Mavity Trophy
Dr. Thomas Cairns & Luis
 Desamero
'Honey Perfume', 'Lavaglut',
 'Mercedes', 'Passionate Kisses',
 'Playgirl'

Jan Shivers National Miniature
 Trophy
Dr. Thomas Cairns & Luis
 Desamero
'Baby Boomer', 'Child's Play', 'Jean
 Kenneally', 'Merlot', 'Michel
 Cholet', 'Old Glory', 'Sweet
 Caroline'

Dee Bennett Memorial Trophy
Peter Alonso Jr.
'Aristocrat', 'Behold', 'Baby
 Claire', 'Glowing Amber',
 'Irresistible', 'Marie Jeanette',
 'Michel Cholet', 'Odessa',
 'Our Little Secret', 'Sam
 Trivitt'

Herb Swim Memorial Trophy
Jeff Stage
'Black Magic', 'Crystalline',
    'Hot Princess', 'Moonstone',
    'Veteran's Honor'

Ann Reilly Memorial Trophy
Dr. Thomas Cairns & Luis
    Desamero
'Day Breaker' (2), 'Rob Roy'
    (2), 'Sweet Nell'

Dr. Griffith Buck National
    Memorial Trophy
Bob & Kitty Belendez
'Abraham Darby', 'Perdita',
    'William Shakespeare 2000'

J. Benjamin Williams Mini-Flora
    Rose Challenge Trophy
Dr. Satish & Vijaya Prabhu
'Aliena' (2), 'Bella Via' (2),
    'Cachet' (2), 'Conundrum' (2),
    'Tiffany Lynn' (2)

GardenWeb Forum Best in Show
    Trophy
Geri & Alan McCarron
'Marilyn Monroe'

NATIONAL HORTICULTURE

Queen of Show
Geri & Alan McCarron
'Marilyn Monroe'

King of Show
Roger & Madeline English
'Crystalline'

Princess of Show
Susan Chan McCarthy
'Lynn Anderson'

Court of Honor
    Ron & Modine Gregory
    'Big Time'

    Carl G. Mahanay
    'Kardinal'

    Bob & Kitty Belendez
    'Moonstone'

Ron & Modine Gregory
'Natasha Monet'

Susan Chan McCarthy
'Signature'

Lynn Snetsinger
'St. Patrick'

Miniature Queen of Show
Joe Smith & Brenda Landers
'Kristin'

Miniature King of Show
Suzanne M. Horn
'Arcanum'

Miniature Princess of Show
Peter Alonso Jr.
'Bee's Knees'

Miniature Court of Honor
Suzanne M. Horn
'Butter Cream'

Suzanne M. Horn
'Conundrum'

Peter Alonso Jr.
'Erin Alonso'

Joe Smith & Brenda Landers
'Fairhope'

William W. Wallace
'Giggles'

Suzanne M. Horn
'Merlot'

Genesis Award
Marianne Thurston
R. roxburghii

Dowager Queen
Ivy Bodin
'Marchesa Boccella'

Victorian Award
Joyce Raymer
'Irene Watts'

Floribunda Bloom
Geri & Alan McCarron
'Pasadena Star'

Floribunda Spray
Col. Philip L. Ash
'Sexy Rexy'

Polyantha Spray
Ron & Modine Gregory
'Chatillon Rose'

Classic Shrub
Col. Philip L. Ash
'Bouquet Parfait'

Modern Shrub
Marilyn S. Wojdak
'Mix 'n' Match'

Climber
Dr. Thomas Cairns & Luis
    Desamero
'Fourth of July'

Three Hybrid Tea or Grandiflora
    Blooms
Jeff Stage
'Veteran's Honor'

Fully Open Hybrid Tea
Lynn Snetsinger
'Gold Medal'

Hybrid Tea or Grandiflora Spray
Susan Chan McCarthy
'Gemini'

11

The Heady Scent
of History

 Punch-drunk with exhaustion after the Spring National, I decided to alleviate my modern-rose overload in the company of old-rose activists. I had anticipated relaxing with a civilized group of history buffs. Instead I found a boisterous crowd of scent addicts. Gardeners who love old roses are reputed to be obsessed with rescuing and identifying long-lost varieties, but after a day spent perambulating the annual Celebration of Old Roses, I can attest that they're actually infatuated with sticking their noses into as many blossoms as they can inhale in the shortest period of time.

The ardor and scent in the El Cerrito, California, community center where the celebration is held were the most intense I had yet experienced. Hosted each Mother's Day by the Heritage Roses Group, this free event brings together antique-rose lovers from all over northern California to show new discoveries, identify found varieties, and shop for yet one more irresistible plant. Unlike a competitive ARS show, the celebration is a simple revelry of roses. Blossoms, grouped by class — noisette, china, hybrid perpetual, and so on — fill a great rectangle of long tables in the center of the room. This is not an orderly display, but a mass of jostling bloom become a gigantic bouquet. Instead of look-alike glass vases, roses bloom from scrubbed jars still labeled with what they had once contained: "Toby's Fresh Ranch Dressing," "Grey Poupon Mustard," "Newman's Own Marinara Sauce."

Vendors around the periphery of the room sell rose-flavored honey, rose jewelry, rose water, rose-shaped lamp toppers, organic rose petal cakes made from "450 varieties of organically grown roses." Spilling out into the courtyard and up the front steps are plant vendors who sell roses, lilies, scented pelargoniums, and more.

Most of all, though, there are *the roses*. Two hours into the event, their scent is dizzying and the floral munificence actually strains my eyes. Other people seem to take the bounty in stride. I spot a blond man in a cowboy hat loaded down with two cameras, a yellow legal pad and pen. He scribbles notes between inhalations. Beside him, a woman in a rose-patterned skirt peers at blossoms through a magnifying glass. A little girl in a pink dress patrols the perimeter of the tables sniffing each rose she can reach, her face a study in concentration. I lean against the old climbers table to rest, nearly causing a 'Devoniensis' in a Vlasic kosher dills jar to spill.

"Tired of roses?" asks a man.

"Just overwhelmed. How about you?"

"Not me. I say, 'Bring 'em on.' My back is giving out, but never my desire for roses."

We scan the floral wealth silently for a moment; then he asks if I've seen the debate in the back of the room. He leads me to a table whose sign reads: UNKNOWN. A hodgepodge of blooms in pickle jars wait for identification. Index cards beside the flowers are scrawled with penciled comments such as "Perhaps 'Russell's Cottage Rose'?" and "Definitely *Rosa roxburghii*."

My guide points to a pearly pink flower.

"It's a gallica. Double — that is very unusual for a gallica." He exhales, causing his narrow mustache to flutter. "But it is definitely a gallica, which narrows it down to two thousand possibilities." He sounds happy.

Opinions on the card beside the rose include "*gallica officinalis*" and "*very like gallica officinalis*" and "*gallica officinalis,* local variant." This does not seem like a debate to me. Then a tall man in blue work shirt and jeans appears at my shoulder and says in a combative tone, "I say it is definitely *gallica officinalis*." I back away.

SUCH DEBATES ARE COMMONPLACE among old-rose lovers. In part, that's because the participants go to great lengths to collect the plants they love. If, for example, you admire the 'Rotes Meer' rugosa in Celeste Woodbury's New Hampshire garden, she's liable to tell you that she stole it. I prefer to say that she rescued it, or in old-rose parlance, she rustled it.

Rustling is a Texas-bred expression for the practice of taking cuttings of roses in order to save them. Rustlers scramble around derelict houses and crawl through old graveyards in search of antique varieties that may have been planted with love but are now forgotten. The practice demands sturdy shoes, a sharp eye, and sharper clippers, as well as labels, water, paper towels, and plastic bags with which to keep the cuttings alive until you can get home to root them.

In the case of the 'Rotes Meer', Celeste rustled the complete plant. "There's a road near here where quite a few 'Rotes Meers' grow wild. I enjoyed driving by them each day; then the state road workers ran them over with their big mowers. When they finally started to grow back, I knew they'd get mowed down again. So I did what any card-carrying rose nut would do in that situation. I drove my car down there in the dark of night and parked a good distance from the site. I walked back with my pail and shovel in hand. I was night-blind, nervous, and sweaty. I dug and tugged, pulling at the fibrous roots to get them loose from the earth. Finally, plop! Several cars passed by as I was digging. So, when their headlights lit me, I stood up and tugged at my jeans, pretending I had just relieved myself! Now I ask you, how dignified is that? And all for a rosebush!"

Celeste and her husband, Jim, live in central New Hampshire, where the growing season is short and the winter is long and cold. Between them, they have seven children, four cats, and a small garden full of antique plants. The varieties may be old, but Celeste is new to their company. She didn't grow any roses until three years ago, when Jim surprised her with four antique alba shrubs named 'Celeste'. Celeste the gardener was astonished by how quickly they grew without any of the fuss that she always assumed roses needed. She bought a few books about the lineage of heritage varieties and was smitten. Much to Jim's regret, the vegetable garden was sacrificed to roses; the fence disappeared in blossoms. Their weekends were transformed into rustling trips. In the summer they hop on the motorcycle and roar off to explore the countryside and search for heritage roses in graveyards and abandoned sites.

"I am always amazed when I find a rose growing in the old cemeteries around here because the headstones often date back to the late 1700s. They've been forgotten, tucked away on some dusty back road. Those are the roses I take cuttings from, because if they could talk, what a story they could tell. When I'm in my garden, I can picture ladies in long dresses and men in top hats of the Victorian era strolling through. I see soldiers plucking a spray of the Minden Rose before going into battle. I imagine Empress Josephine admiring her vast collection at Malmaison."

THREE HUNDRED MILES south of Celeste in Dutchess County, New York, Lily Shohan likes to picture what was happening when her ancient Rose of Paestum, known as 'Autumn Damask', first sprouted. It's an extraordinarily fragrant, twice-blooming variety that she thinks might be two thousand years old.

When Lily began to grow roses fifty years ago, heritage varieties were nearly impossible to find, except in an old cemetery or Great Aunt Somebody's garden. Times have changed. "There was a time when I could have grown, in my own garden, every old-rose variety offered by the nurseries in this country. I couldn't begin to do that anymore. There are roses out there that I've never heard of." Today old-garden roses and antique-looking modern roses are trendy. In 2005 the American Rose Society asked the Heritage Rose Foundation to create a garden of antique varieties for the new ARS headquarters in Shreveport, Louisiana. And Marilyn Wellen, who broke tradition by becoming only the second woman in one hundred years to serve a term as ARS president, also broke the unspoken tradition of old-rose/modern-rose antagonism by attending the Heritage Rose Foundation conference that preceded the Celebration of Old Roses in El Cerrito.

John Mattia refers to Lily as the "grand lady of old garden roses." He also calls her a "legend in her own time," which makes her simultaneously chuckle and groan. She is an enthusiastic, opinionated, white-haired, cane-toting dynamo with a bad hip and a habit of laughter.

While most exhibitors of modern roses will say, "*Look* at this," when showing you a flower they love, old-rose people tend to push you head first toward a blossom and say, "*Smell* this." Stephen Scanniello, president of the Heritage Rose Foundation, says that Lily wields a "wicked cane" when she wants you to inhale. He may lack Lily's cane, but he does as much deep breathing as other old-rose advocates; he describes his favorite flower as "intoxicating."

Lily nods when I report Stephen's opinion; her gardens are a testament to its truth. She is eighty, semiretired from a career in insurance and not at all retired from her two hundred or so plants. Her favorite is the first one she ever grew, a fragrant damask named 'Celsiana'. Hybridized around 1732, the shrub has strongly perfumed pink double flowers that bloom in June. In the winter she grows the tea rose 'Safrano' indoors, where its apricot lemon blossoms and heady scent warm her home despite snow outside.

When I met Lily, she told me that she once grew over 450 plants, but since her seventy-fifth birthday, she says, she has been scaling back.

"Now if I decide that I hate a rose, I let it go and don't replace it." This is said resolutely. The problem is that catalogs continue to clog her mailbox and rose friends continue to send her cuttings. I recently received this e-mail from Lily concerning her efforts to scale back her garden: "Was just out planting a rose today. I have three more to put in and four or five more coming this week. Am opening up a new bed on the lower level of the garden, so am not sure that the 'scaling back' is working all that well."

Scent and beauty delight her, but it's the age of the antique
varieties in her garden that amazes her. Wouldn't it be wonderful, she asks, if her 'Autumn Damask' really *is* two thousand years
old? Roses passed along as cuttings are always clones, or pieces of
the mother plant. That is why the Rose of Paestum in Lily's garden, which has been passed cutting by cutting since the Mother
Paestum first appeared, is very old indeed. But how old?

Not necessarily two millennia, says Brent Dickerson, a renowned historian whose massive volumes, *The Old Rose Infor-
mant, The Old Rose Advisor,* and *The Old Rose Adventurer,* are
bible/encyclopedias in the OGR world. After consulting with
knowledgeable Latinists, he learned that the description of Paestum translates as "the rose gardens of twice-bearing Paestum,"
which simply meant that Paestum was a verdant place with lots
of roses. Thus, writes Dickerson, who loves a good rose story,
but loves the truth even more, "It would appear, then, that the
supposed reblooming roses were simply lush-growing plants
blooming over an extended season along with everything else in
Paestum and Campania due to the favorable climate."

He does report that in 1580 the French essayist Montaigne reported seeing a rose grown by Italian Jesuits that bloomed every
month of the year. They evidently gave him a cutting. So Lily's
two-thousand-year-old rose might at least be five hundred or so
years old, which isn't bad.

"It's the living flesh of an ancient rose," says Lily, her blue eyes
alight. "That's what gets me — history alive in *my* garden." We
lean back in our chairs to consider what was happening five hundred, or perhaps two thousand years ago, when her rose first appeared. I can't help but grin.

"Cool," I say.

"Cool," she echoes.

Lily's garden is as enthusiastic as she is. Buxom shrubs spill over fences and cascade beside a stone wall. Six-foot behemoths crowd the edges of her property in shades of pink and cream. On a warm June afternoon, Lily's flowers scent the neighborhood. A particularly sweet climber envelops a corner of the farmhouse in wedding white. Lily discovered the plant beside an old house near her property. She compared the plant to descriptions in Mrs. Frederick Keays's old-rose handbooks from the 1930s and '40s and identified it as *R. alba* 'Maxima'. Originating in the 1500s, it used to be called the 'Jacobite Rose' because its blossom was the badge of those who supported the Stuart kings after their 1688 exile.

Old roses offer the chance to turn a corner and find yourself in the past. The realization that you can grow the same rose — *literally* — that Josephine Bonaparte grew at Malmaison in 1800 produces shivers of disbelief. Talk about a space-time continuum. Antique-rose lovers have as much fun ferreting out the provenance of their plants as weekend genealogists do researching family history. It's educational — and it is full of good, gossipy stories. When Donna Fuss of Elizabeth Park in Connecticut showed me a sprawling centifolia called 'Maiden's Blush', she said that the original name of the six-hundred-year-old variety was 'Cuisse de Nymphe'. "I translate that as 'sensuous nymph with tempestuous thighs,'" said Donna. "Well, the Brits felt, 'Oh my, we can't have that,' and changed the name. But as far as I am concerned, she wasn't blushing at all; she was having herself a good old time."

Lily doesn't mind that her two-thousand-year-old rose might be a five-hundred-year-old youngster, because she is as partial to the intricacies of identification as Brent Dickerson. While DNA testing has made rose classification easier, it is an expensive process reserved for the most important cases — varieties whose identification will spur enough sales to pay for the DNA tests. Meanwhile, field classification satisfies in a contentious way.

"I got a rose from someone quite a few years ago that was an obvious 'Double Cinnamon'," says Lily. "The guy who sent it to me says, 'No, it's not.' But a 'Double Cinnamon' is what it is: reddish shoots, spicy fragrance, small, mauve pink blossoms. Every time I see him he says 'no' and I tell him that he's wrong." She chuckles. "But my favorite variety right now is the rooted sucker of 'De la Grifferaie' that an elderly lady from Maine gave me." 'De la Grifferaie' is a massive shrub with scented, double carmine blossoms. "I have it wrapped around a pyramid in my front garden. I get applause from passersby for that rose. It looks fantastic."

I wished for Lily's forthright company when I visited the Heritage Rose Garden in San Jose, California. The garden, which comprises the largest public collection of rose varieties in the Western Hemisphere, includes OGRs from all over the world, as well as a special collection of California found roses. Four thousand five hundred plants encompassing thirty-five hundred varieties jostle one another in arc-shaped beds and trail into gravel pathways, vying for one's attention.

I was standing in front of a rosebush when a tall woman in a floppy hat walked up, pointed at the plant, and asked, "What's this?"

If Lily had been there, she would have told her immediately, but I had to open the garden's ninety-six-page rose-locator catalog and find marker 8-6 in section P — Reblooming Old Garden Roses.

" 'Rose du Roi'."

"No!" She shouted at me. She truly did shout. "That is *not* 'Rose du Roi'." — pronouncing the last word as "roy." She turned on me and said with a let-me-make-this-very-clear ferocity, " 'Rose du Roy' is red."

These were pink.

A young man, slung about with cameras, appeared at my right shoulder. He leaned forward to peer at the heavily scented blossoms. "I certainly don't know what it is."

"Well, I don't know what it is either, but I know what it isn't!" The woman in the floppy hat stalked off toward section K — Chinas and Teas. Without turning around, she called back, "Actually, *I* think it's 'Souvenir de la Malmaison'." The young man shrugged and lifted a camera up to his face to photograph the mystery rose.

I flopped the loose-leaf catalog shut and watched two women kneeling nearby with red Felco pruners, paper towels, plastic bags, and bottles of water.

"Okay, this is what we want," said one woman to the other. "A hybrid bourbon." Whereupon she snipped off a six-inch piece of stem, wrapped the end in wet paper towel, and dropped it in a bag. "Cut only the spent blooms," she warned as her companion unlocked her own Felcos.

Even so, what do they think they're doing? This isn't an abandoned farmstead or overgrown roadside. These women are rustling roses in a public garden. I backtracked toward section O — Once-Blooming Old Garden Roses and almost collided with a tall bearded man whose neck was encircled in a long striped muffler. The temperature in the garden must have been

80 degrees F. He opened his arms wide in symbolic embrace as he addressed a fragrant, pink, six-footer.

"'Fortuné Besson' my old friend. You're not winter hardy, but you always grow back."

I scampered to Mel Hulse, volunteer director of the garden. Not to worry, he reassured me. He knew exactly who was cutting what because they had asked his permission.

"Course, we have people who come in here and dig up roses; that's not right." He paused as a plane roared overhead. The garden is directly underneath the flight path of the San Jose International Airport. A tall man, Mel tilted forward as he talked, leaning on a thick wooden cane. He was dressed in pale khakis, plaid cotton shirt, thick white socks, and worn Birkenstocks.

"All kinds of things go on in this garden. I came in one day and found black slacks and panties on the bench. He gestures toward a wooden bench currently occupied by two women, one of whom is saying, "I told him, 'You gotta look at more than the bloom darling, look at the bud!'" Her companion nods and offers, "It's the color of flesh that a cosmetician paints on a corpse."

Mel shook his head, "There were ten more panties scattered about on different rosebushes. Never did figure it out."

Colonel Mel Hulse is twice retired — first, from the U.S. Air Force as a pilot and, second, from Lockheed Martin as a systems engineer. He fell in love with flowers as a child in his mother's big front-yard garden. He fell for roses when he was stationed in Seville, Spain, and his gardener asked for permission to create a rose garden.

"I didn't know what most of them were, but I fell in love with them. Then I fell into fascination with them. This garden is

designed to show how roses began and where they might be going next. They are so old and there is so much variation among
them. We have a rosebush that is three inches in diameter; that's
its full-grown size. And I have a rose at home that is busily climbing a walnut tree."

Mel helped dig in the garden's initial planting of thirty-five
hundred roses in March 1995; he has volunteered here ever since.
As we toured the grounds, the scent of blossoms was head-
swimmingly heavy. Some of the plants were labeled. Some marked
with donation tags. I paused in front of an 'Autumn Damask',
thinking of Lily, and spotted a metal tag inscribed, "This beautiful rose reminds us of you, Annie. We love you." Most of the
thousands of plants, though, are marked only with their location
number and must be identified — or not — using the garden's
guidebook. Not that one needs the guidebook in order to wander, inhale, and appreciate.

As I meandered along the paths, breathing deep and dodging
blossom-laden canes, I particularly admired the found roses —
varieties that have been rustled from some California hillside,
identified, and given safe haven. This garden is refuge for the
plant that may have guided Christopher Columbus to safety.
Legend has it that on October 11, 1492, while becalmed in the
Sargasso Sea, one of Christopher Columbus's crewmen picked a
spray of roses from the water. This gave them hope of land, and
when the wind picked up, Columbus's three small ships sailed
forward toward the Americas. Apocryphal or not, it makes a
good beginning.

Most of the thirty-five native North American rose species are
small to medium-sized shrubs with five- to ten-petal white, pink,
or scarlet blossoms. They bloom abundantly in early summer and

sporadically through the rest of the season. In general, they are hardy, adaptable, and tough.

English colonists concentrated on simple survival during their early years in the New World, which may be one reason that decorative plants receive less mention in the first reports than do edible flora and fauna. Yet roses had medicinal value, so we do hear something of them. In 1606 Captain James Smith reported that the Indians of Virginia planted roses, as well as sunflowers and grapes, around their villages.

Native Americans used the bark, root, canes, leaves, and flowers of roses to treat everything from head colds to stomach worms. Fresh leaves of *R. pisocarpa* (gray cluster rose) stuffed into moccasins cured athlete's foot, while a poultice of *R. acicularis* (prickly rose) leaves made bee stings less painful. An infusion of prickly rose bark used by the Indians of the Northwest induced vomiting, which is useful if you've eaten the wrong thing. Such an infusion was also drunk after childbirth by the Iroquois of New York, who may have had stronger stomachs. Everyone, meanwhile, ate fresh rosehips in late summer and dried them for winter snacks.

In 1621 Edward Winslow, who had managed not to die during the Plymouth Colony's first winter of "great sickness," ventured out to see what bloomed in the New World. He reported, "Here are Grapes, white and red, and very sweete and strong; also Strawberries, Gooseberries, Raspas [raspberries]. Plums of three sorts, white, black, and red, being almost as good as a Damson. Abundance of Roses, white, red, and damask, single but very sweete indeed."

After a winter of snow and starvation, Winslow was undoubtedly pale, dirty, and shaky on his feet. Imagine him scouting the forest edge within sight of the nineteen "Meersteads and

Garden-Plotes of those who came first." He holds tight to his musket, steps carefully to avoid the strawberry plants, picks a strong sweet grape, then leans over to inhale the abundance of roses. He must have felt such relief at that moment, such a lift of the spirits. The beloved emblem of his homeland grew in the New World.

"Of all flowers, Methinks a rose is best," Shakespeare wrote for all of us. We adore roses so much that we have made them the universal symbol of love. And just as we pursue love despite its complexity, it may be the contradictions of the rose that keep us in its thrall. Haunting sweet scent from a thorny briar. Velvet petals on a plant that can prick. Tender new growth, the color of rubies, on a cane that draws blood from the unwary.

The roses that Smith had seen in 1606 were probably *R. virginiana,* a freely suckering medium shrub with scented, bright pink flowers and cheery round hips. In 1724 settlers sent it back to England. It was the first native American species cultivated in Europe, and pleasingly, it was a hit. Yet *R. virginiana* was one of the few native North American roses that made it socially in Europe. *R. arkansana, R. blanda, R. californica, R. carolina, R. michiganensis, R. nutkana, R. pisocarpa, R. woodsii* — encouraged by the floriferous habits of such evocatively named species, British and European growers tried with little success over the years to breed them with ever-blooming china and tea rose hybrids.

As for Winslow's report of damasks — wouldn't it be wonderful if the species of rose transplanted from Syria to England in Crusaders' saddlebags had been in the New World all the time? Wonderful, but unlikely. Despite the mysterious power of wind and birds, Winslow probably meant that he saw a scented pink blossom that reminded him of the much loved damask.

One more hint of what was growing wild in America appears in Meriwether Lewis's diary entry of Saturday, June 8, 1805. The Lewis and Clark expedition was in the Missouri Territory: "In adition to which [the river] passes through a rich fertile and one of the most beatifully picteresque countries that I ever beheld, through the wide expance of which, innumerable herds of living anamals are seen, it's borders garished with one continued garden of roses." (The spelling is his.)

While explorers collected specimens of incompatible American roses to display as curiosities in Old World botanic gardens, new Americans imported their Old World favorites as fast as possible. In 1655 a Dutch visitor wrote home to say that "the Netherlanders have introduced . . . white and red roses of diffcrent kinds, the cornelian roses, and stock roses." Just north in New England in 1674 John Josselyn said that "English Roses" grew "very pleasantly" in American gardens. And in 1681 William Penn famously arrived to establish Philadelphia with so many roses that visitors soon remarked on the city's aromatic gardens. Beginning in 1731, the Penn family rented out parcels of land for the annual fee of one red rose per parcel.

Fittingly, our first president also loved roses. Washington's 1792 order from Pennsylvania's Bartram Botanic Garden included *R. pennsylvanica* — "flowers monthly from May 'till Novembr" he wrote in the margin of the order, and *R. palustris,* or swamp rose, which he noted incorrectly would "grow in any soil and situation." He wrote that he favored "Wild Roses for hedges."

Washington also loved to increase his stock of hybrids. Yet

despite persistent folklore, Washington did not create and name a rose for his mother. The 'Mary Washington' is a vigorous, white, double-flowered shrub that does grow around Mount Vernon. Mary's son may well have wanted to create it had he known of it. But the rose is a noisette, a variety that would not be bred until twelve years after Washington's death.

MEL AND I FOUND the noisette 'Champneys' Pink Cluster' among other reblooming varieties in section P at the Heritage Rose Garden. Five feet high, its long canes spilled over our feet and dropped pink petals from a wealth of blooms. 'Champneys' Pink Cluster' was the first rose hybridized in the New World. As the story goes, in 1811 John Champneys, a rose-loving rice planter in Charleston, South Carolina, was given an *R. chinensis* named 'Parson's Pink' by his neighbor Philippe Noisette, superintendent of the South Carolina Medical Society's Botanical Garden. Champneys crossed his gift with an unnamed musk rose. From the resulting hips, he grew a pretty pink rambler that he named for himself. 'Champneys' Pink Cluster' has bunches of blush pink, scented double blossoms that bloom once per season. (If you want to grow a bit of American history, it's still available from specialty nurseries.)

Champneys presented Noisette with seedlings of the new rose. Noisette harvested the seedlings' hips, sowed the seeds, and from them developed his own new variety, 'Blush Noisette'. It looked much like its parent, except that it bloomed continuously through the season. Recognizing a winner, Noisette sent seedlings to his brother Louis, a nurseryman in Paris, who is credited with using them to create a new class of roses — the noisettes.

Mel leaned stiffly down to retrieve a pink blossom. "Roses offer everything. You can be interested in their history, the biology of how they grow, in raising all of them or growing just one variety, exhibiting them, writing about them, finding them in the wild." He paused, breathless. "And, of course, they are beautiful." He rapped the cane on the ground.

12

Rescuing Roses
with Ruth

 America's first hybridized rose has Ruth Knopf to thank for its survival. Ruth founded the Noisette Study Garden in Charleston, South Carolina. She has a genteel manner, honeyed South Carolina accent, and a will of iron. All are invaluable attributes when spearheading the creation of a botanic garden. When she isn't improving the garden, she consults for private and public rose collections. And she famously travels with pruners so that she can rustle, or "pilfer," as she calls it, endangered roses whenever necessary.

Driving through Charleston's back streets with Ruth, I realize that America's first family of roses isn't confined to the study garden. "Look, see that?" She points to a tumble of dark pink rose in front of a ramshackle three-story wooden house. " 'Blush Noisette'. We have tried three times to get a cutting. But the owner refuses. She says 'no' just to be mean." Ruth sighs. A block along, she slows in front of another rundown house. "But we do have cuttings from that." She points to a white rose beside the front stoop. Her smile is triumphant.

Ruth's passion for America's roses began with the simple desire to plant pink flowers that she remembered from childhood around the house that she and her husband moved into as newly-weds. She was told that the roses she described were probably old-garden varieties.

"I had no idea that such things existed," says Ruth. She thought that old roses inevitably led to modern hybrid teas.

Then came the lucky day when a friend invited her on an Open Garden Day tour. In Newberry, South Carolina, Ruth saw a pink bloom that matched her memory. She asked the owner, Ruth Westwood, where she might buy it.

"Oh fiddlesticks dear, that's a found rose," said Westwood. "Come back tomorrow. I'll give you cuttings."

"But I don't know what to do with a cutting," Ruth protested.

"You come back and I'll teach you everything you need to know."

Ruth Westwood proved to be an excellent teacher. Ruth was soon searching abandoned farmsteads, overgrown cemeteries, and roadside ditches for roses. These were roses she could afford; roses with history, which she loves; roses that reminded her of a happy childhood.

How did she know what she was looking for?

"Well, you read," she says in a gentle, admonitory voice. "You look at the growth pattern, foliage, blossoms, buds. Gradually you learn to tell one variety from another."

Ruth makes it sound easy, but when I had used *The Field Guide to Rose Characteristics* at the Heritage Rose Foundation conference, I had struggled to identify the potted rose on which I'd practiced. Goodness knows how I'd manage in an overgrown cemetery.

What is the bush form? asks the field guide, whose questions and line drawings were developed as a way to systematically re-cord data about found roses. Is it *suckering, vase shaped, arching, rounded-upright, sarmentose (flexible canes),* or *climbing (rigid canes)*? Faced with an unidentified shrub in a container, I was grateful for the drawings. I circled "vase shaped" and moved on through new growth color, which was "bronzy" and mature cane surface, which was "gray green."

"Prickles" gave me pause. Were they *setaceous (bristly), straight (needle-like), falcate (sickle-like), hooked, dilated (wide), declining (angled down), ascending (angled up),* or *geminate (twin)*? For a while, my rose had "falcate," "dilated," and "declining" prickles, but upon close examination, "declining red" won out. I couldn't decide between "serrate" and "serrulate" leaf margins, mostly because the line drawings looked almost identical. And I dithered for ages on petal form before choosing "cuneate," which means wedge.

Perhaps it was information overload, but my attempt to identify the form of the blossoms' sexual parts reduced me to near hysteria. Were the tall yellow styles in the middle of the blossom *united on a column* or *free*? Were they *villous (soft hairs), pilose (stiff hairs),* or *glabrous (smooth)*? I figure that if I had to identify roses in the wild rather than during a Heritage Rose Foundation conference, I would manage one plant per day and come home with a poison ivy rash. Ruth's proficiency in the field awes me.

She took cuttings of the varieties she found in those early years and rooted and identified them. Those that she couldn't classify were given study names to describe where she'd found them. Then she planted the roses around her home. Hundreds of roses.

Thorns prick even the most fragrant tales. In 1989 Ruth's husband died. He had been a minister. Ministers don't own the houses they live in, so Ruth left their flower-bedecked home and moved to a beach cottage on Sullivan's Island off Charleston.

"I took the roses that were in pots. But after I settled in, I thought to take cuttings of the others. When I went back with my pruners, they'd been bulldozed." Ruth's wide blue eyes become wider. "Mounded up in a great dead pile. All those roses. Just gone."

We drive in silence for a bit before she breaks the hush. "But rose people are there for each other." Over the years she had given cuttings of almost all her plants to friends. Gregg Lowery and Phillip Robinson, owners of Vintage Gardens, a heritage-rose nursery in Sebastopol, California, had received many hundreds of cuttings. Now they, in turn, made cuttings of the roses they had grown from her plants. She glances at me. "So all was not lost. It was just the act of bulldozing that I don't understand."

Despite the happy ending, her voice reverberates with a mix of pain and fury when she describes her lost flowers. Yet to portray the Noisette Study Garden as Ruth's revenge may be incorrect. It is a horticultural laboratory, as well as a place to keep historic varieties safe from bulldozers. The idea for the garden began in the 1990s, when Ruth noticed that America's first rose, 'Champneys' Pink Cluster', and its noisette cousins were gradually disappearing from their birthplace. At the same time she realized that many of the remaining noisettes blooming in alleys and backyards were misidentified pretenders. She decided to create a scientific garden in which the real noisettes could be separated from the false, and the true lineage of America's rose preserved. With the help of JoAnne Breland, Charleston's superintendent of Horticulture, Ruth and noisette-loving rosarians planted the first study roses in 1999.

The same variety grown under different conditions can develop variations in growth habit, flowering, and leaf color. So identifying roses in the field — something Ruth has spent years doing — can be a confounding experience. Ruth says that they may never be able to establish that a particular plant is the original 'Champneys' Pink Cluster' and another is not. But with careful observation and some DNA testing, they should be able to determine that a 'Champneys' Pink Cluster' sold by one nursery is the same one sold by a second nursery, and the same as a found rose, 'Jane Doe', but different from a rose sold as 'Champneys' Pink Cluster' by two other nurseries. Ultimately, Ruth hopes to encourage nurseries to rename misidentified plants.

Roses that constitute the study garden now fill fifteen long beds around a large reflecting pool in Charleston's Hampton Park, which is bordered by the Citadel military academy on one side and city greenhouses on the other. The park, with clipped flat lawns, graceful trees and tidy beds of annuals, is a vast and orderly space that contrasts with the encircling tumble of old roses. However well tended the beds — and these are beautifully maintained — antique roses can be large and disorderly. They fountain into the park's raked gravel path and bump each other with thorny canes. I am reminded of Tommy Cairns's comment that he keeps his own collection of twenty-five OGRs "out of the way where I can tolerate their unruliness." The Noisette Study Garden roses are in-your-face plants.

The roses are not labeled because many of the oldest noisettes were stolen from this public garden almost as soon as they were planted. "People know that some of these are rare, you see," says Ruth. "Greedy people and" — she searches for the right word — "covetous people."

We have forgotten to bring a map, so Ruth identifies from memory as we amble. A sprawling 'Blush Noisette'. A fountain of 'Nacogdoches Noisette', collected from a cemetery in Nacogdoches, Texas. "I think that it's not a pure noisette, but a noisette and china cross. Never mind that, though. It's always in bloom. And look at that foliage, no disease. We don't spray, you know."

A massive yellow musk named 'Claire Jacquier' welcomes us with deep perfume. A bed with 'Mary Washington', the fragrant, pink and white noisette named for George Washington's mother. We pass a bramble of 'Champneys' Pink Cluster' that is even bigger than the one I saw at the San Jose Heritage Rose Garden. "Notice how the primitive noisettes like Champneys' have small flowers. Much more like a wild rose than a hybrid." The simple pink blossoms mingle with those of its neighbor, a tea/noisette cross. "That's 'Jim's Fence Corner', a found rose." Ruth smiles beneath the brim of a pink ribbon hat. "Lovely study name, don't you think?"

I imagine Jim, whose fence must have disappeared every summer in apple-sweet pink petals. He may have pruned the rose back a bit each year and poured a bucket of manure slop on its roots every once in a while; or he might simply have left it to grow, unsupervised, where he or a bird had planted it. I am certain that he appreciated its annual gift of flowers and hips. He may even have loved it as much as early settlers loved the precious cuttings that they nurtured on long voyages. Able to carry only a few belongings in their boats and wagons, thousands of families packed a living reminder of loveliness alongside the bare necessities. One finds such roses still blooming beside wayside taverns where they stopped. They color long-abandoned wells and broken wagon wheels in pink and white. They flower like yellow sunrise around the doorways of the frontier homes those families built. And along old cart tracks through the woods, they still offer comfort to those who didn't make it. A tilted tiny gravestone — Abigail, aged 2 years, 4 months, 1 day — and beside it the red rose of never-ending love that blooms again each June.

"Roses are remarkable," I offer.

"Oh my, yes." Ruth's pink hat dips as she nods. "The rose is the toughest plant in the world."

13

Clarence's Charges

 Tough is what matters in Maine-grown roses, even for Clarence's Rubbermaid-container varieties. In early November the annual shift of plants does not seem feasible, for Clarence and I cannot stand together in his two-car garage without colliding with something sharp, dusty, or potentially sticky. The space is filled with carpentry tools, garden tools, a lawn mower, and bottles and bags of potting mix, fertilizers, pesticides, and fungicides.

Three weeks later, though, he calls to announce that the garage is clean. I head right over.

"Clarence?"

"Yeah! I'm in the basement. Come on down, but mind your head."

Across the small kitchen, cheerful with floral wallpaper, oak cabinets, and a corner table invisible beneath rose society newsletters and plant catalogs. Down steep but sturdy stairs to two warm dry rooms. The room on the right holds a washer and dryer, a deep metal sink filled with khaki pants and hot soapy water, a stack of precisely folded white towels, clean rag mops leaning rag head up beneath the stairs, a wall of shelves colored with the fruits of Clarence's vegetable garden. Quarts of red tomatoes, emerald pints of pickle relish, burgundy beets, rosy half pints of raspberry jam, sunshine quarts of corn.

Clarence appears around the base of the stairs.

"'Seneca Chief'," he says. "Same corn that my dad grew when I was a kid."

He is dressed in work-stained khakis, long-sleeved green T-shirt and the rose-colored wool cardigan that he was wearing when we first met. The green and black baseball cap with pink lettering that he bought at the Spring National in San Diego perches on his head.

"Notice how the kernels are whole?" The quart jars appear to be full of yellow candy corn. "I hate crushed corn." His shoulders actually wriggle with distaste. "So I invented this thing — it's a grapefruit knife that I modified — that cuts out the kernels without crushing them."

He runs a hand along the yellow ribbon of glass jars, then beckons. We cross into the work room, edging past waist-high tool racks, rolls of copper wire, bins of bolts and flanges and screws and . . .

"I sorted the garage last night and I found all this junk," he says in a satisfied tone.

He digs into a mound of small hexagonal washers and nuts, much as a boy might dig into a bag of marbles. "Look at these fittings. When I got them all down here last night from the garage, I thought, 'Oh geez, I don't know where I got all these. No one could ever use them.' But this morning I decided that they're like a security blanket. Twenty years from now, they might come in handy."

Seventy-five-year-old Clarence expects to be making things when he is ninety-five.

Right now, we head outside to see his newest construction: three chest-high boxes encased in silver tarpaulin to cover roses that bloomed riotously all summer. Clarence built a twenty-five-foot-long box to cover the hybrid teas planted under the back windows. He dumped five wheelbarrow loads of decomposed leaves into the box, laid plywood on top, wrapped the box in silver tarpaulin, and draped the tarpaulin with ropes secured on each end by window-sash weights. Remember the weighted ropes designed for his second-generation rose-winterizing boxes? The ones in which the roses shriveled from dehydration? Same weighted ropes; better boxes.

"When I uncover next year, I'll just mix the leaves into the soil."

Figuring out how to winter-protect his in-ground roses was "the easy part," says Clarence. "Had to cover the container roses, too. That's harder."

"But your containers go into the garage."

"Won't all fit. Had to leave room for *some* other stuff in there." Before I can ask, "What other stuff?" he hastens to another silver box. "Good thing that I had lots of plywood."

Clarence has laid forty container roses, alternating head and foot, on their sides on the ground. He built a four-foot-high plywood container around them and laid more plywood directly on top of the pots. He has topped the plywood sheets with his "newest innovation" — pine needle pillows.

"I sucked up pine needles from my neighbor's yard with my vacuum cleaner. Got enough to fill four huge construction bags.

Then I bought" — Clarence falters as he admits to purchasing something new but soldiers on — "I bought small plastic bags with drawstrings. I filled them with the pine needles and laid them down on the plywood."

He unwraps the end of a tarp-covered box so that I can see inside. The bristle of pruned, dormant canes looks well, cozy, beneath its pine-pillow comforter.

"I haven't had much success with the black containers in these boxes." He sounds regretful and intrigued. "They survive, but not well. The big thing is to provide enough insulation to keep them going, but make it easy for me to do." He pokes a white plastic pillow. "This way, I won't have to clean out the pine needles in the spring. They'll already be in bags."

He has covered the bags with quarter-inch foam laminated with white polyethylene, put on a plywood cover, wrapped the box in tarpaulin, and draped the entire creation with roped window-sash weights. Clarence has said he loves hybrid teas because they are classically beautiful, but standing there with him, watching him, I think he may love them more because they are such a challenge to overwinter in Maine.

Many northern rosarians relish the effort required to keep their plants safe from winter blasts. Donna Fuss laughs when she describes running outside in Connecticut after a dire forecast to "plop covers on 150 roses." Maine Rose Society members love to discuss the relative merits of compost versus soil as insulation in below-zero weather. Participants on the Garden Web rose forum vote for bales of straw. Ah, the lengths we go to protect the fragile creatures with which we've fallen in love.

Lois Ann Helgeson has dispensed with all those solutions.

Instead, she keeps 565 roses blooming in New Brighton, Minnesota, by burying them. "By the time I'm finished in the fall, it looks like a little graveyard in my garden." Lois Ann is a ceramic artist, which explains her knowledge of soil. "Both my interests are dirty."

She uses two burial methods. The first, known as the Minnesota Tip, was demonstrated at a national rose convention by Lois Ann's friend Dr. Henry Najat, who grows over one thousand roses near Madison, Wisconsin. To perform the Minnesota Tip, you tie up the top of the plant, dig a trench beside it, tip the plant over into the trench, and bury it. Not to worry, said Lois Ann, roses are quite flexible. For years, she did this plant by plant: tie up rose, split grass, tip rose, close up grass, and mark it with a little wooden stake so she could find and identify it again.

Two hundred fifteen of Lois Ann's 565 roses survive Minnesota's brutal winters without complaint. She Minnesota Tips half of her 350 tender roses. The rest she digs up completely, bundles into chicken-wire cages and buries in eight-by-three-foot trenches that are eighteen- to twenty-four inches deep. She does this for all except two special climbers: 'Secret Garden Musk' and 'Dorothy Perkins'. The 'Dorothy Perkins', from a woman who died recently, is over a hundred years old; 'Secret Garden Musk' is an "indulgence" that Lois Ann bought at the ARS Spring National in San Diego. For these roses Lois Ann digs ten-foot, rather than eight-foot, trenches.

She lays contractor blankets across all the trenches and covers the blankets with seventy to one hundred bags of oak leaves. Each fall, she puts out a sign — LEAVES WANTED — and bags appear. In the spring she empties them wherever she needs mulch.

Lois Ann bought twenty plants at the Celebration of Old Roses in El Cerrito. When I asked how she planned to get them all back to Minnesota, she just laughed. She prunes them back hard, ties up their canes, dumps out half the soil from the pots, wraps them in plastic, and puts them in her suitcase. I was dumbstruck with admiration. Lois Ann shrugged. "I always come home with plants. They're my souvenir."

"And your husband is supportive?"

"Well, he's tolerant. Usually, it's roses. Sometimes, I'll have camellias and Japanese maples thrown in."

"Camellias in Minnesota?"

"They come indoors over the winter." She hesitated at this point. I remember worrying that she might feel she had shared too much and resolved to trade her tales of my own gardening excesses. "I grow the Japanese maples in pots, so I bury those just like the roses. I also grow dahlias. I'm the national chair for publicity for the American Dahlia Society." Her dimples deepened as my eyes widened. "But roses are my passion."

At the end of the season Clarence's passion comprises a thorny welter in the center of the garage. Blue rolling Rubbermaid trash bins are jammed together, plastic side to plastic side; but Clarence has pruned the canes so that they cannot touch and damage each other. On Clarence-made tables and shelves around them is all the stuff that didn't make it out of the garage. More plywood and foam insulation, plant sprayers, bottles of dark liquid, green plastic plant ties, sander and router, coils of rope, a yellow hardhat, and empty Cool Whip and Folgers coffee containers, which are perfect for mixing brews and potions.

A peg board along one wall is outlined with the tools that hang on it — hammers, mallets, staple-gun, handsaws. At least fifty of Clarence's version of the Bridges/Wright Bloom Protector gleam from poles strung between the rafters.

We push a long compost thermometer into a front-row container so that Clarence can monitor the temperature of the containers during the coming winter.

"So that's that," I say. "You fit all the extra roses into the garage."

"Not really. I rolled a few down to Mrs. Homan's garage." Gracious and pretty at ninety years old, Claire Homan is treasurer of the Maine Rose Society

Forty-four roses in Clarence's garage, twenty in Mrs. Homan's.

He picks up another thermometer. "Come on."

We walk down the road, turn in at the second driveway. Clarence's roses are neatly ranged along the left side of Mrs. Homan's one-car garage, leaving enough room for her small car on the right. As we push the second thermometer into the soil around a rose, Clarence explains that he has stored them here as an experiment.

"Not because you can't fit them all into your garage?"

"That, too." He is unabashed. "But I might learn something new. After Mrs. Homan has driven, the car in the garage is warm for a while. And I think that more sun falls on this roof than on mine." He peers up into the rafters. "I want to see if these roses survive the winter differently than the ones in my garage."

Back in Clarence's house, I point to the catalogs that color his kitchen table with temptation.

"Are you going to order anything?"

"Oh, I don't know. I'm not sure if . . ." Clarence's voice drifts toward inaudibility.

"You're mumbling!"

He grins. "I know. I can't say it out loud yet. Last year, I bought ten, maybe fifteen, just to buy some roses. This year . . . well, I don't need any roses."

Clarence shifts the catalogs about, picks one up, sets it down. He offers me a glass of water. As he turns his back to fill the glass, he says, "Heard there's a hybrid perpetual that looks like a hybrid tea. Might have to give that a try."

A man who stores roses in the garage, co-opts his neighbor's garage, and crowds his back yard with huge silver boxes does not need more plants — not even a hybrid perpetual that masquerades as a hybrid tea. But that is not the point. Clarence's roses offer him friendship with people whom he would otherwise never meet and they keep him interested in the future.

This anticipatory attitude may be why I've succumbed to Clarence and to all the other people I've met in the rose-obsessed world. They exude an enthusiasm for life that is infectious. They also evoke a spirit of make-do and can-do that is vanishing in a culture cluttered with purchases that never quite satisfy.

It may be that people who coax recalcitrant flowers into bloom are naturally persistent. Those who breed their own striped pink miniature are born problem solvers. Perhaps rescuing a long-lost variety or designing a blossom protector from a juice bottle creates self-confidence and optimism. Whatever it is, the results are energizing.

During the next few months, rosarians all over the country will peruse catalogs and visit midwinter shows. They will share information about irresistible varieties and pass along rumors — someone has found healthy stands of endangered *R. minutifolia* — someone else has grown sun-loving 'Hot Cocoa' in the shade. They will sharpen their pruners and scissors, ready their rustling supplies and grooming kits, submit their orders. This time, they are certain, their selections will be stronger, hardier, rarer, more fragrant, more colorful, more exquisitely shaped. This time, their roses will be winners.

You are responsible, forever, for what you have tamed.
You are responsible for your rose.

—Antoine de Saint-Exupéry

Several rose classification systems are in use around the world. One of the most popular was devised by the American Rose Society in cooperation with the World Federation of Rose Societies. The classification schema reflects the botanical and evolutionary progress of the rose.

Genus: *Rosa*

Species Roses

Often called wild roses, species roses are the parents of modern roses. Single petal (4–11 petals) and once blooming, they range in size from 2 to 20 feet. They are listed according to their Latin name. Species roses rated "excellent" and "outstanding" by the ARS are:

- *R. banksiae* var. *banksiae*
- *R. rugosa* var. *rubra*
- *R. banksiae* var. *lutea*
- *R. rugosa* var. *alba*
- *R. setigera*
- *R. gallica* var. *versicolor*
- *R. moschata*
- Kiftsgate

Old-Garden Roses (OGRs)

The ARS defines old-garden roses as those hybridized prior to 1867, the year that 'La France', the first hybrid tea, was introduced. The most popular classes of OGRs are:

- Alba
- Ayrshire
- Bourbon and Climbing Bourbon
- Boursault
- Centifolia
- Damask
- Hybrid Bracteata
- Hybrid China and Climbing Hybrid China
- Hybrid Eglanteria

Modern Roses

Modern roses are those developed since 1867. The accepted classification is based on the plants' growth habit:

- Floribunda and Climbing Floribunda
- Grandiflora and Climbing Grandiflora
- Hybrid Kordesii
- Hybrid Moyesii
- Hybrid Musk
- Hybrid Rugosa
- Hybrid Tea and Climbing Hybrid Tea
- Hybrid Wichurana
- Large-Flowered Climber

(continued)

Genus: *Rosa* (*continued*)

Species Roses	Old-Garden Roses (OGRs)	Modern Roses
• *R. gallica*	• Hybrid Foetida	• Miniature and Climbing Miniature
• *R. rugosa*	• Hybrid Gallica	
• *R. glauca*	• Hybrid Multiflora	• Mini-flora
• *R. roxburghii*	• Hybrid Perpetual and Climbing Hybrid Perpetual	• Polyantha and Climbing Polyantha
• *R. gallica* var. *officinalis*		
• *R. laevigata*		• Shrub
• *R. roxburghii* var. *normalis*	• Hybrid Sempervirens	
• *R. virginiana*	• Hybrid Setigera	
• *R. hugonis*	• Hybrid Spinosissima	
• *R. elegantera*	• Moss and Climbing Moss	
• *R. spinosissima*	• Noisette	
• *R. banksiae*	• Portland	
• *R. palustris*	• Tea and Climbing Tea	
• *R. sericea* var. *pteracantha*		

GLOSSARY OF ROSE CLASSES

Alba — Spring-blooming, scented, white-blossomed plants that are upright, often climbing, with dense, disease-resistant blue-green foliage.

Bourbon — Beloved in Victorian England, these were the first repeat-flowering roses bred from the hybrid china class. The class includes shrubs and climbers with glossy foliage that is susceptible to blackspot and was named for the location of the first members of the class: Île de Bourbon in the Indian Ocean.

Boursault — Small class of thornless, scentless, rambling roses that flower profusely. Named for the amateur horticulturalist who bred them during Napoleon's reign.

Centifolia — Dutch roses named for their hundred-petal pink and purple blossoms; also called cabbage roses. Hardy, large, shrubby plants that bloom briefly, but extravagantly, in spring.

Damask — Ancient group of roses brought west from the Middle East by the Crusaders. Big, hardy, thorny plants that have clusters of fragrant white and pink blossoms followed by large hips.

English/Austin — Since 1970 British nurseryman David Austin has been breeding old roses with modern roses to create these old-fashioned-style plants with better disease resistance and much longer bloom period.

Explorer — Extremely hardy, repeat-blooming pink and crimson roses bred from rugosas by Agriculture Canada.

Floribunda — Hardy and disease resistant, these compact, shrubby roses were a 1930s cross between hybrid teas and polyanthas. The bright, clustered blossoms flower throughout the season.

Grandiflora — Considered a subclass of hybrid tea, these are large, upright plants whose large, hybrid tea-shaped blossoms grow in clusters like a floribunda.

Hybrid china — Tender, small shrubs with clusters of spicy pink and red blossoms that bloom over an extended period. Disease-resistant foliage.

Hybrid gallica — Before the nineteenth century, the gallica was the most frequently cultivated rose. Medium, spreading shrubs with dull, resinous-scented leaves, prickly canes, and vibrant, scented crimson and purple flowers that are often striped.

Hybrid musk — Developed in the early twentieth century by an English clergyman from *R. multiflora* and *R. chinensis.* Continuously blooming large shrubs with huge clusters of scented, small, pink, white, and pale yellow blossoms. In a long season, the plant will climb.

Hybrid perpetual — First bred in France in 1837 from crossing hybrid chinas with portlands and bourbons. A favorite in Victorian England, this is a tall, hardy plant whose huge pink, red, and white blossoms sit down among the foliage. Blooms in June and sporadically throughout the season.

Hybrid tea — Originally produced by breeding long-stemmed tea roses with large-flowered hybrid perpetuals, the hybrid tea is the world's most popular florist and exhibition rose. Three- to six-foot high, upright shrubs with long canes topped by large, high-centered flowers that bloom in every color except blue. Fragrant, or not, depending on the desire of the breeder. Many hybrid teas are not winter hardy.

Miniature — Naturally dwarf roses that range in height from five inches to ten-foot climbers; most are one to two feet tall with small leaves and dwarf blossoms shaped like hybrid teas or floribundas. Long-lasting cut flowers.

Mini-flora — In the 1970s Maryland hybridizer J. Benjamin Williams copyrighted the name "mini-flora" to describe an ever-blooming, hardy rose he had created that was larger than a miniature but smaller than a floribunda.

Moss — First introduced from Holland to England in 1596, the moss is thought to be a sport of the centifolia rose. They resemble centifolias in their habit, except that their buds and upper stems are covered with tiny scented glands that increase the roses' perfume and create a mossy look.

Noisette — In 1811 American rice planter John Champneys created the first American-bred rose, 'Champneys' Pink Cluster' by crossing a china rose with a musk rose. The result was a large, hardy shrub with abundant clusters of white, lemon, and pale pink blossoms that bloom late in the season. Cuttings passed to Philippe Noisette were passed again to Philippe's brother Louis Noisette, a French rose breeder, who developed the class known as noisette.

Polyantha — Created in 1875 by crossing a china rose with a dwarf, re-peat-flowering *R. multiflora,* polyanthas are compact shrubs that bear many clusters of small white and pink flowers that bloom throughout the season.

Portland — Compact, bushy shrubs that flower in late spring and autumn with scented burgundy and crimson blossoms set low in a cluster of leaves. Hardy and easy to grow, they are a china-damask cross. Bred in England in the early 1800s, and sent by the Duchess of Portland to France where they were further developed by Josephine's gardener at Malmaison.

Shrub — A class of roses that do not fit into other categories and/or a descriptor of many classes of bushy roses.

Spinosissima — Also known as 'Scot Rose' or 'Scotch Rose', these hardy, low- to medium-growing shrubs have prickly stems and fernlike, dis-ease-resistant foliage. Single-petal, pink, white, and yellow blossoms bloom in May and June. Related to the 'Burnet Rose' and the 'Wild Irish Rose'.

Tea — Originally a cross between wild tea roses (*R. gigantea*) and *R. chinensis,* these delicate roses were brought to England from China in 1810. Very tender, with pastel, urn-shaped blossoms that have a tealike scent, the roses were popular in the late 1800s. Crossed with hybrid perpetuals to create the hugely successful hybrid tea class.

GLOSSARY OF ROSE TERMS

Basel break — A new rose cane growing from the bud union.

Blackspot — A fungus that forms dark spots on leaves; causes weakness and defoliation.

Bloom or **Blossom** — A rose flower that has passed the bud stage.

Blown — A bloom that has opened beyond exhibition stage, that is, half to three-quarters open.

Bud — A rose flower whose petals are not yet open.

Bud union — Enlarged growth above the root that indicates that the rose was grafted onto rootstock.

Cane — A main stem of a rose.

Cultivar — Another term for plant variety.

Cutting — A piece of stem used for propagation.

Disbudding — The removal of flower buds in order to allow other flower buds to grow larger.

Double — A bloom with seventeen to twenty-five petals in three or more rows.

Exhibition form — A rose that is half to three-quarters open with a high center and symmetrically arranged petals.

Exhibitor — An individual or member of a team that has entered a rose in a competitive rose show.

Grafting — Joining the stem or bud of one plant onto another.

Grooming — Improvement of a rose specimen by an exhibitor.

High centered — The shape typical of a hybrid tea bloom; long inner petals forming a narrow peak above the bloom.

Hip — The fruit of a rose that contains the seed; forms at the base of a blossom after the petals have fallen.

Hybrid — The result of cross-pollinating two rose varieties.

Hybridizing — Another term for plant breeding, or joining two plants to create a third.

Pruning — Removing parts of a plant to improve appearance, eliminate damage or disease, and/or produce new growth.

Rosarian — A person who grows roses knowledgeably.

Semi-double — A bloom with twelve to sixteen petals in two rows.

Single — A bloom with five to twelve petals in a single row.

Specimen — A rose blossom or cluster of blossoms on a stem.

Sport — A genetic mutation that creates a spontaneous change in a plant.

Spray — Three or more blossoms that grow near each other on a stem.

Variety — A named rose cultivar, for example, the hybrid tea named 'La France'.

Books

Beales, Peter, ed. *Botanica's Roses: The Encyclopedia of Roses.* New York: Ball, 1998.

Bernhardt, Peter. *The Rose's Kiss: A Natural History of the Flower.* Washington, DC: Island Press, 1999.

Christopher, Thomas. *In Search of Lost Roses.* Chicago: University of Chicago Press, 2002.

Goor, Asaph. *The History of the Rose in the Holy Land throughout the Ages.* Tel Aviv: Pel Printing Works, 1981.

Harkness, Peter. *The Rose: An Illustrated History.* Buffalo, NY: Firefly Books, 2003.

Hedrick, U. P. *A History of Horticulture in America to 1860.* 1950. Reprint, Portland, OR: Timber Press, 1989.

Leighton, Ann. *American Gardens of the Nineteenth Century.* Amherst: University of Massachusetts Press, 1987.

Martin, Robert. *Showing Good Roses: A Complete Exhibitor's Guide.* Pasadena, CA: Roseshow.com, 2001.

McCann, Sean. *The Rose: An Encyclopedia of North American Roses, Rosarians, and Rose Lore.* Mechanicsburg, PA: Stackpole Books, 1993.

Morris, James McGrath. *The Rose Man of Sing Sing.* New York: Fordham University Press, 2003.

Scanniello, Stephen. *A Year of Roses.* Rev. ed. Nashville: Cool Springs Press, 2006.

Scanniello, Stephen, and Tania Bayard. *Climbing Roses.* Upper Saddle River, NJ: Prentice-Hall, 1994.

———. *Roses of America: The Brooklyn Botanic Garden's Guide to Our National Flower.* New York: Henry Holt, 1990.

Shepherd, Roy E. *History of the Rose.* 1954. Reprint, New York: Earl M. Coleman, 1978.

Winterrowd, Wayne, ed. *Roses: A Celebration.* New York: North Point Press, 2003.

Web Sites and Rose Forums

www.ars.org
Web site of the American Rose Society

www.gardenweb.com/forums
The forums on roses, antique roses, exhibiting, miniatures, and propagation and exchange are active and informative.

www.helpmefind.com/roses
Online rose encyclopedia

www.heritagerosefoundation.org
Web site of the Heritage Rose Foundation

members.tripod.com/buggyrose/
Web site of Baldo Villegas, ARS member and expert in rose diseases and pests

www.rdrop.com/~paul/
Paul Barden's Web site of old-garden roses

www.rogersroses.com
Online rose encyclopedia

www.rose.org
Web site of the All-America Rose Selection program

www.rosemania.com
Online rose-gardening retailer, which also sells John Mattia's digital rose photographs.

www.roseshow.com
The Web site of Bob Martin, author of *Showing Good Roses.* Reports the results of ARS district and national rose shows.

www.scvrs.homestead.com
Web site of the Santa Clarita Valley Rose Society, offering a wealth of informative articles. Readers can also subscribe to their award-winning
newsletter, "Rose Ecstasy," which is edited by Kitty Belendez.

www.worldrose.org
Web site of the World Federation of Rose Societies

ACKNOWLEDGMENTS

This book could not have been written without the help and advice of
many people. First and foremost is Clarence Rhodes, who started the
whole thing off. Without Clarence and the generous, impassioned people
of the rose world, this book would not exist. Thank you all for letting me
visit with you.

Amy Sutherland encouraged me to write a book. Jane Chelius helped
me identify and polish the topic. Harley Manhart bravely read and edited the first version. Priscilla Grant listened to each revision and kept
me moving forward whenever doubt assailed. Bob Krug read every word
many times and critiqued them with clarity and kindness. Antonia Fusco
pushed me to make it the best it could be. And, through it all, my amazing
family applauded. I am more grateful than words can express.